WE
STILL
HERE

WE STILL HERE

PANDEMIC, POLICING, PROTEST, & POSSIBILITY

MARC LAMONT HILL

Edited by Frank Barat
Foreword by Keeanga-Yamahtta Taylor

Haymarket Books
Chicago, Illinois

Published in 2020 by
Haymarket Books
P.O. Box 180165
Chicago, IL 60618
773-583-7884
www.haymarketbooks.org
info@haymarketbooks.org

ISBN: 978-1-64259-453-9

Distributed to the trade in the US through Consortium Book
Sales and Distribution (www.cbsd.com) and internationally
through Ingram Publisher Services International (www.
ingramcontent.com).

This book was published with the generous support of Lannan
Foundation and Wallace Action Fund.

Special discounts are available for bulk purchases by organizations
and institutions. Please call 773-583-7884 or email
info@haymarketbooks.org for more information.

Cover photograph information on page 119.
Cover design by Rachel Cohen.

Printed in Canada by union labor.

Library of Congress Cataloging-in-Publication data is available.

10 9 8 7 6 5 4 3 2 1

*To my father, Leon M. Hill Jr., who continues to teach
me daily lessons about courage, resilience, humility,
and unconditional love.*

and

*To my daughter, Anya Coleman-Hill, whose brilliance,
passion, and warrior spirit
inspire me to keep writing and fighting
for the world she deserves.*

CONTENTS

THE RISING

In the five decades since the last spasms of the Black insurgency, there have been periodic reminders that taking racism out of the law (to the limited extent that has even happened) has not been enough to remove it from our society. Usually these incidents come in the form of the pent-up rage unleashed by a riot or a catastrophic event that shows how history hangs onto the present, sometimes like a nightmare from which we cannot awaken. In our recent past, Hurricane Katrina shocked the nation out of a colorblind stupor to remind us all that to be poor and Black in the United States is to be at the rock bottom of a rigged social order. There was the mass murder of nine Black parishioners at Emanuel African Methodist Episcopal Church in South Carolina, just weeks after the Baltimore Rebellion raged in memory of murdered Freddie Gray. This was months into the emergence of the Black Lives Matter movement; a bitter rejoinder to the delusion of a post-racial society. This was the rhythm of a post–civil rights United States: periods of quiet and invisible suffering, punctuated with violent, syncopated outbursts in demands of belonging, justice, home.

But in the long end to legal racism, there has never been anything like the wretched, lost spring of 2020. The ravages of the novel coronavirus and its disease, Covid-19, and the deadly hum of racist violence inflicted on the bodies of Breonna Taylor and Ahmaud Arbery made it feel as if winter would never end. The mystery of this novel virus soon gave way to a dismal familiarity: premature death conjured by the preexisting conditions of racism, inequality, and their bitter harvests. Within a matter of weeks of the virus's arrival, it was coming into sharper focus that Black and Brown were going to bear the brunt of this disease. The ease of its transmission—and the impossibility of its prevention for the poor and working class—was bound to be a disaster in slow motion. What did "social distance" mean for people who could not work from home and whose jobs were instantly, and in Orwellian hyperbole, declared "essential"? Jobs just essential enough to keep Black women on the front lines, but not essential enough for hazard pay, personal protective equipment, or living wages that could pull these women away from the front lines of a generational public health crisis.

This slow-motion horror sped up while the grim body count began. Black people were dying at rates faster than anyone else in the country. In city after city, Black rates of infection and death were substantially higher than their proportion of the population. By the end of April 2020, it was clear that this new virus would have an outsized impact in

Black communities because of the ways in which racism exposed ordinary Black people to the virus and broke all of the systems that might alleviate its impact. Black people were more likely to live in crowded housing, to not be properly insured, to suffer preexisting health ailments that could make the virus deadly. Of all the reminders that the United States remained a deeply racist and unequal society, long after the laws that nominally abolished racism had been written, Covid-19 was devastating.

As thousands of Black people were dying because racism rendered their lives expendable, the violence of the police showed again that their lives were also disposable. The public execution of George Floyd on a Minneapolis street in broad daylight showed that even in the midst of unprecedented national disaster, the police could be unmoved and continue their assaults on Black people.

But if the killings of George Floyd and Breonna Taylor lit the fuse, Covid-19 was the incendiary device waiting to explode. Across the country, tens of millions of people participated in the June uprisings that were a direct response against police racism and violence were also unmistakably against the social, economic, and political system that turned Covid-19 into the third leading cause of death for Black people in 2020.

The rebellion, as uprisings often do, introduced the viewpoint of the rowdy masses into the staid and stale governmental debates about insufficient levels of public aid. The rebellions have fundamentally changed the nature of the conversation by reviving the frameworks of systemic and institutional racism, as activists called for the defunding of the police and investment in genuine public services and programs. They have created a model for social transformation in the United States in ways profound and necessary.

Marc Lamont Hill offers critical insights into the whirlwind that pandemic and racism have reaped. *We Still Here* appears at a time of intense study and debate about how we got here—and, most important, how we get out. Politics, history, strategy, and tactics are all that our side has. Read this book, and we'll see you in the streets.

—Keeanga-Yamahtta Taylor
August 25, 2020

INTRODUCTION: HOW SHALL WE DIE?

Right after George Floyd was killed, on May 25, 2020, organizers in Philadelphia pulled together a huge protest. We were more than two months into the Covid-19 pandemic, and most of the people I knew had been home and socially distanced. But now my phone was blowing up. It was time to get out and make our voices heard. In all my adult life, there had hardly been a major action in my city I hadn't participated in. As I considered the situation, I had to confront this reality: we live in a country built on individualism and selfishness—and in this hour, our ability to survive, my ability to survive, was going to hinge on the actions of countless random others. I didn't worry about the activists I knew. But they weren't going to be the only ones out there, and too many Americans had shown little regard for what was needed from every single one of us: to make our own selves uncomfortable in order to ensure another's life. That's what wearing masks is all about. You protect me; I protect you. It was a high-stakes call to become Martin Luther King's "beloved community"—and immediately.

I had to make a calculation. I was a forty-one-year-old Black man living through a pandemic that was disproportionately killing Black people, regardless of age. I honestly wasn't sure that I could go and come back healthy. If I went to a protest and was exposed to the virus, would I survive? Would I wake up alone on a hospital ventilator, fighting for my life?

More than anything, I worried that if I became ill, it would delay my being able to see my father. He is ninety-two and frail. In February 2020, we had to rush him to the hospital, and afterward he was transferred to his nursing home. In both places, our family had circled around him in the days before everything shut down. We could visit and sit with him. He was weak and the prognosis was grim, but at least we were together with the man who had loved my mother for half a century. Who had given everything he had to ensure my siblings and I would thrive. A Black man who cut a path through the brutal terrain of Jim Crow Georgia, the state that came in second in lynchings only to Mississippi. My father survived the violence of his home state, the US Army, and the UpSouth police in the era of Frank Rizzo, who beat him unconscious in the 1970s. He became an educator who raised educators, and I needed to see him again, touch his hand. If he had to die, how could he possibly be allowed to go alone, in a hospital or nursing home, where he lay too weak even to hold a phone up and hear our voices telling him how much we loved him?

I'd prayed I'd be able to see my father when the country began opening up again. But things kept getting worse, and the hospitals and nursing home were overrun, making it hard to even get information on his status, leaving me and my mother and siblings just to wonder and worry. And in that first breathless push of pre-summer, when George Floyd pleaded for his breath, for his life, I was left making these very real and human choices that so many Black people were making at the same time.

The thing that we have to do to keep us alive could also be the thing that kills us.

I wanted to help resist the state and its consistent efforts to kill us. I wanted to join in solidarity with this younger generation of activists as they called not just to defund but abolish police. I wanted to stand with them as they tore down statues to White supremacy. I wanted to support their amazing and courageous work, but I couldn't because I was worried that I could get sick or, worse, that I could get someone else sick. This conundrum in many ways represents what it means to be Black in America: *In what way am I going to resist death today?*

Being Black and made medically vulnerable, we're more likely to die from coronavirus. Being Black and in the streets, where we are targeted, we are more likely to be killed by those whose job description is to keep us safe. That contradiction prompted me to try to make sense of this moment in real time. Whether it's protesting state violence in the streets of Minneapolis or New York or Philadelphia; whether it's in an overrun hospital or nursing home; whether we are discussing a frontline worker providing medical care or a frontline family member providing everything else; the thread runs through: we must account for the many ways that Black people are forced to undertake simultaneous fights for our lives and the lives of those whom we love.

I sat down with my friend and comrade Frank Barat, a longtime French activist whom I knew from our international solidarity work. I chose Frank because he had a perspective that was needed, sitting outside the United States.

We had a series of conversations on everything from Covid-19's specific impact on Black people to the ways that capitalism helped create the conditions for premature death. We pull apart "Corona capitalism" and unpack the politics of disposability that write off people sitting in prisons, immigration detention facilities, nursing homes, and other places of confinement. We explore the Spectacle of Death. What does it mean for us to see George Floyd die this terrible public death? What does it mean for us to see Black people dying, constantly, on Twitter and other social media? In looking at police violence, here and elsewhere, when we call for nonviolence, are we in fact instead calling for the state to have the exclusive right to be violent? Most important, we consider what it means to resist and re-create the world guided by a Black feminist politics that prioritizes the fundamental value of all lives.

♦

Today is August 11, 2020. I still have not seen my father. Coronavirus may not have killed him, but it has taken him

from us in another very real way. Like many of you reading these words, our family lives with the anxiety of this
moment, the sword of death hanging just above. We live
with the shame that accompanies our not being able to care
for him ourselves. And we live with a specific grief: I don't
know if the last time I saw my father was the last time I will
ever see him. Wrestling with that along with everything
that is happening in the streets is overwhelming beyond
description.

So much has been taken, but not everything.

What this moment has taught us is that we have the
ability to radically reimagine and reshape the world. Since
March 2020, we have watched a new generation of activists,
building on everyone who has come before them, shift the
public conversation further to the left. It's not that we didn't
talk about prison and police abolition in the 1990s or 2000s,
but there's something interesting and different when members of Congress are calling for it. Although many still dis-
agree with our radical vision, there is finally an actual debate,
one that takes us down to the core of it all.

Victory is closer than ever.

It's not enough just to recount the things that have happened in this crazy year of 2020. We must analyze the deeper
conditions and structures that allowed 2020 to happen. It's
not enough to respond to Donald Trump's incompetence or
the extraordinary grief that people are living with in a time
of pandemic. We must come to understand everything that
brought us here. This is what young organizers in the streets

are demanding. That is what everyone living in the time of pandemic, policing, protest, and possibility must reckon with.

That is why I wrote this book.

—MLH
Philadelphia, PA

PREEXISTING CONDITIONS

Frank Barat: *Covid-19 represents arguably the biggest global public health crisis of the last century. How are you studying it as a social scientist and critic?*

Marc Lamont Hill: When dealing with a pandemic, our attention is quite reasonably fixed on issues of infection, sickness, treatment, and death. For this reason, we tend to look to doctors, epidemiologists, and other medical experts for concrete insights. But this moment cannot be examined purely through the lens of medicine or "hard" science. We must also look to history, social science, journalism, and other ways of investigating the world. Like any other phenomenon, Covid-19 must be examined within the proper social, cultural, political, and economic context. This doesn't just satisfy an abstract academic curiosity. It helps us to understand where we are, how we got here, and how we can arrive at transformative solutions.

This question of "how we got here" is an important one.

Absolutely. In the most direct terms, we can say that the Covid-19 pandemic in the United States is the direct result of gross mismanagement by President Donald Trump. While it is certainly not his fault that the virus existed, Trump failed at nearly every opportunity to mitigate or even acknowledge its threat.

In January 2020, even as the World Health Organization declared the novel coronavirus a global health emergency, Trump insisted that we had nothing to worry about. His decision to restrict travel to China may have allayed xenophobic anxieties but occurred far too late to actually slow infection rates. In February 2020, even as he reluctantly put together a coronavirus task force, Trump continued to tell the country that the infection rates would quickly be reduced to zero. By the time the Trump administration took serious policy measures to contain the coronavirus in March, the crisis had become infinitely harder to control.

You've described Trump's actions as an example of "mismanagement," which suggests that he made mistakes. But the context you're describing seems more intentional.

I don't want to speculate on Trump's intentions, nor can I comfortably say what he was thinking. What I can say, without question, is that Trump's mistakes were entirely preventable.

First of all, Trump was left with clear pandemic guidelines by the Obama administration. At the end of his second term, president Barack Obama's team of scientific advisers left Trump with a sixty-nine-page "pandemic playbook" that offered concrete strategies for responding to a crisis like Covid-19. The playbook discussed the importance of obtaining personal protective equipment (PPE), having a clear and unified communication system with the public, and, most of all, an urgent all-out government commitment to eliminating the pandemic as quickly as possible. The evidence clearly shows that Trump failed to follow any of these suggestions.

Beyond ignoring Obama, President Trump also failed to keep pace with the US's peers. As other countries purchased PPE and testing kits, Trump stubbornly insisted that such measures were unnecessary. Instead of engaging in rigorous tracing procedures, Trump actively peddled the dangerous lie that the antimalarial drug hydroxychloroquine could treat or even prevent Covid-19.

There are many reasons to consider for Trump's refusal to properly address the pandemic. Perhaps Trump's visceral hatred of and one-sided competition with President Obama prompted him to reject any advice from Obama's team. Given Trump's refusal to admit mistakes or apologize for harm, it is also possible that he simply could not bring himself to change course. Or maybe Trump simply did not want to shut down the economy, which was an unavoidable consequence of creating a national stay-at-home order. As an economic populist during a reelection year, Trump surely understood how a struggling economy would undermine his chances of defeating Joe Biden.

All of these answers are plausible. Unfortunately, given Trump's consistent dishonesty, there is no way to determine with any certainty what actually happened. What we know for sure, however, is that better choices were made available to him. His failure to make those choices contributed largely to the current crisis.

Let's stay with this question of "how we got here." Beyond Trump, how should we understand the deeper social conditions that created the pandemic?

Well, we can begin with the way that the virus spread. For perhaps the first time in modern history, a global health pandemic was spread from the privileged down to the poor. Rather than originating in urban ghettos, Covid-19 spread through the physical movement of economic elites. Many people traveling to ski in Colorado, do business in China, shop in Italy, or study in Germany traveled back to their home countries as carriers of the virus. For this reason, it should be no surprise that early infections around the world were concentrated within wealthy neighborhoods. This created a dangerous and false narrative that only the wealthy were susceptible to the virus. In fact, in places like Central Mexico, Northern Nigeria, and Mumbai, India, the coronavirus was literally being called "rich man's disease." And, in many ways, it was. As always, though, rich people's problems quickly became poor people's burdens.

When the wealthy became ill, domestic workers, caretakers, and service industry employees were soon infected as well. They took coronavirus back to their communities, which didn't have access to the same level of resources to protect people from the virus. It's no surprise that the tables quickly turned and that the overwhelming majority of coronavirus-related deaths have been of poor Black and Brown people.

Experts said that the biggest protection from the virus was social distance.

There's no doubt that social distance is the best way to protect from Covid-19 and many other illnesses. The public conversation on social distance, however, was far too simplistic. Too often, media outlets, politicians, and health officials failed to acknowledge that establishing social distance isn't merely an individual choice, like wearing a condom or covering your nose when you sneeze.

Of course, everyone should try to social-distance. We all can be intentional about avoiding people, places, and situations that produce epidemiological danger. But in real life, social distance isn't just a physical, geographic, or spatial measure. Social distance is also an index of privilege. Who has the ability to create social distance? Who has the resources to sustain social distance? The answers to these questions reveal deep structural issues.

Economic power enables social distance. Spacious homes, gated communities, and private modes of transportation have enabled the wealthy to establish social distance without significant disruption to their lifestyles. For example, being able to "self-quarantine" at home without placing neighbors, friends, or family at risk requires a built environment that is nearly impossible to create without money.

The power to create social distance is also linked to the social and economic power of Whiteness. Even when there is no immediate crisis, the powerful have designed cities in ways that keep Whites separated from Blacks, as well as other groups that historically have been deemed undesirable, including Italians and Jewish people. These racist practices were codified in law through covenants, redlining, road construction, and other legal practices. Underneath these practices were racist beliefs about these groups that included their being carriers of disease. This has led to a self-fulfilling social prophecy, as minoritized populations have often been forced into densely populated ghettos.

"Sheltering in place" is a luxury of the privileged. Decades of racist government housing policy, combined with unstable job markets, have forced people to share their homes with more people than is desirable or safe. These homes are often situated within densely populated neighborhoods or housing projects, making social distancing at home impossible. This is why news stories and internet memes of poor Black people hanging outside during the municipal "stay at home" orders are so deeply dishonest. For some people, hanging on the corner or sitting in the park is a far safer option than staying in, especially if someone at home is sick.

Working from home is another way that we were told to create social distance. Since the beginning of the pandemic, however, low-wage workers were forced to work jobs that placed them on the front lines of risk. People working gig-economy jobs—Uber drivers, retail and service-industry workers, and other folk facing financial precarity—were left with no choice but to risk their lives every day in order to survive. These people were transformed into "essential workers" without any commensurate wage increases, hazard pay, or other financial incentives to risk their lives.

Meat processing plants, for example, were ordered to stay open, as the US government deemed food and agriculture to be one of twelve essential industries required to stay open despite the federal guidelines for everyone to stay home. The Trump administration determined that they should not only remain open but also operate at high efficiency in order to avoid national food shortages. The consequence of this decision was that large numbers of factory employees were forced to work in dense indoor spaces in order to maintain high production rates. In many cases, these workers did so without proper PPE. It is hardly surprising that at the Tyson Foods factories alone, more than ten thousand employees around the country tested positive for coronavirus. And what did the company do? It kept production going. To add insult to injury, Tyson quickly reverted back to their pre-pandemic absentee policy. This meant that staying home to avoid infection could cost you your job. Workers had to choose between earning a living and protecting their lives.

What are some other structural factors that were in play beyond social distancing?

Let's start with medical care. We do not live in a country with universal health coverage. If we did, everyone would have universal access to promotive, preventative, curative, rehabilitative, and palliative care simply because they were human beings. Instead, we live in a country that offers the option of universal health *insurance*. This means that our ability to access quality health care is directly tied to our ability to pay for it. Many people who are unemployed, or otherwise in financial crisis, cannot obtain regular checkups, tests, early diagnosis and treatments, and other forms of medical care that are proven to enhance health. These are also the very things needed to better prevent, fight, and recover from Covid-19 and other illnesses.

Food insecurity is also an important but under-addressed issue. More than 37 million people in the United States are food insecure or lack access to the types of foods that promote an active and healthy life. Every day, millions of people inside the richest nation in human history have to travel miles from home to get fresh foods, or they have to make inhumane decisions like choosing between preparing a reasonably healthy meal and buying medicine. Food insecurity makes people far more susceptible to high blood pressure, diabetes, obesity, and other illnesses that compromise their ability to survive and recover from Covid-19. This insecurity was only made worse when many neighborhood stores closed their doors during the pandemic. Now, folks have to travel even farther to buy food, which raises transportation costs and increases exposure to illness.

Economic vulnerability also undermines access to quality education. In our current system, school funding is determined by property tax revenue. This means that, effectively, we have accepted a social contract that consigns poor people to inferior schools. As sociologists have demonstrated for decades, poor quality education reproduces social inequality. As a result, as sociologist Paul Willis once noted, working-class kids end up getting working-class jobs—the very jobs that make it harder to access living wages or quality health care. This "education debt," to borrow a phrase from Gloria Ladson-Billings, expanded after the pandemic began. Wealthy independent schools and well-resourced public schools offered online instruction with little interruption to the school year, while many poorer public schools lacked the infrastructure to offer meaningful instruction to students.

Imagine a six-year-old child whose family lives below the poverty line. This child attends a public school that is forced to close due to Covid-19. That child no longer has access to two of her three meals a day, which were provided through a free breakfast and lunch program. She is also now home all day, but her parents are forced to work to provide food and avoid eventual eviction. How do they afford child-care for the forty new hours per week that the child is home? This predicament places them in greater precarity, as they have to take on considerable health and economic risk in order to respond to an unforeseeable crisis.

And what about the child? Without reliable internet access outside of her parent's cell phone, she will struggle to access school instruction. Without access to instruction, especially at an early age, she may struggle to remain on grade level for reading. If she is not on grade level for reading, she is far less likely to graduate. If she doesn't graduate, she is far more likely to end up with the same socioeconomic status as her parents—or worse. In this regard, Covid-19 didn't merely spotlight the profound inequalities within our current social arrangement. In many ways, it made them worse.

African Americans account for 60 percent of the dead in this crisis, while they account for about 13 percent of the overall population in the United States. What does this number tell us? What does it say about race today?

These chilling numbers are a reminder that we must not only study the Covid-19 crisis through the lens of class but also think about the very specific way that race is implicated. This is where Ruth Wilson Gilmore's analysis of racism is indispensable. Gilmore challenges us to think about the ways that racist systems do not merely deny certain groups access to social goods or fair treatment. She dares us to consider how racist systems render certain groups vulnerable to "premature death." The overrepresentation of Black people in the Covid-19 death toll provides a perfect example of this.

While Covid-19 infection and survival can be linked to economic vulnerability, we must consider that Black folk are disproportionately vulnerable. Black people remain near the top of every index of social misery and hover close to the bottom of every measure of social prosperity. Black families have a net worth ten times less than their White counterparts. We are consistently denied access to housing, health care, education, food security, and living-wage jobs. These realities create the conditions for Black vulnerability.

But Black vulnerability is not reducible to a class analysis that simply attributes Black suffering to our status as being disproportionately poor. Black people are forced to navigate the world in starkly different ways than their White counterparts. Poor White people are treated differently than poor Black people within courtrooms, hospitals, and labor markets. Middle-class Black people still confront racialized injustice—in the form of structural inequality as well as microaggressions—during work, school, and interactions with police.

So, yes, class is indispensable to an analysis of the Covid-19 pandemic. But it does not tell the full story. We live in a nation built on what Cedric Robinson referred to as "racial capitalism." This "democracy" is indebted to the creation of a racialized group—enslaved Africans—whose labor could be exploited for the purpose of building and fortifying the nation-state. This practice of racialization was informed by a White supremacist logic that viewed Black bodies as sites of wealth extraction rather than humanity. Centuries of this exploitation have created what scholar Eddie Glaude calls a "value gap," or the belief that White lives are simply worth more than others. It is this gap that allows the United States to completely shut down when faced with the prospect of mass death, only to quickly reopen once it became clear that poor Black people were the ones most at risk of dying.

So, yes, we should be mindful of our individual health. We should absolutely make responsible choices whenever possible. But it would be a gross mistake to attribute Covid-19 infections to individual choice and biological destiny. We must never ignore the fact that our choices are shaped, and constrained, by the social realities in which we find ourselves.

At the end of the day, Black life is not inherently valuable in this country. And Black death does not constitute a crisis. We are reminded daily that our worth is directly tied to the needs and interests of the powerful. This reality, by far, is the most important and influential preexisting condition.

CORONA CAPITALISM

The economic realities of Covid-19 are quite serious. How do you make sense of what is happening in the United States?

While surviving Covid-19 is the biggest priority, the economic challenges related to the illness cannot be overstated. Given the relationship between poverty and infection rates, the people most likely to be infected are also the most likely to have precarious employment. As a result, many people who got sick were fired from their jobs. By April, nearly half of all people in the country indicated that someone in their household had been laid off or let go because of Covid-19. Some who held onto their jobs were hourly employees with no sick leave or options to work from home. As a result, they were unable to earn money as they recovered. And given their lack of quality health care and other protective factors, their recovery times were extended. So as they recovered from Covid-19, many people found themselves in long-term financial peril.

And the economic dangers were not merely for those who were sick. Within six weeks of the US economy slowing down in mid-March, more than 30 million were newly out of work. By the end of May, that number reached 40 million. By the end of June, the unemployment rate had skyrocketed to more than 47.2 percent. In April, nearly a third of Americans reported that they could not afford to pay their rent. One study predicted that Covid-19 would push more than 21 million additional Americans into poverty.

And the economic devastation of Covid-19 is even more extreme when we look globally. The June 2020 Global Economic Prospects Report shows that the pandemic could push 71 million people into extreme poverty. The overwhelming majority of the new poor will be concentrated in already vulnerable areas, with almost half in South Asia and more than a third in sub-Saharan Africa.

But the story of Covid-19 is about so much more than the devastation of the world's vulnerable. While this devastation should be our most pressing concern, it can only be properly addressed and repaired with a proper understanding of the forces, systems, institutions, and ideologies that constitute the current moment. This requires an examination of Corona capitalism and how it shapes, reflects, and exacerbates the current moment.

What is Corona capitalism?

Corona capitalism refers to the economic conditions and institutional arrangements that made the vulnerable more likely to experience premature death during the Covid-19 pandemic. Corona capitalism also speaks to the ways that human crises are exploited by the powerful, who coordinate with governments to create policies that enable them to profit during such moments.

Corona capitalism isn't a new mode of production or even a new iteration of capitalism. Rather, it describes how centuries of racial capitalism and decades of neoliberal economic policy not only created the conditions for the Covid-19 pandemic but also informed our legal, economic, medical, ecological, cultural, and social responses to it. While these responses bear a strong resemblance to those of previous junctures, they also bear the specific imprint of the current moment. As we stand in the rubble of Covid-19, we are unable to deny the dangers and limits of the current economic arrangement as it relates to the state, the environment, and the lives of the vulnerable.

Corona capitalism exposes the danger of living within a White supremacist capitalist empire. In the United States, being poor and Black makes you more likely to get sick. Being poor, Black, and sick makes you more likely to die. Your proximity to death makes you disposable. Your disposability makes you more exploitable. Within this condition, race is not incidental or a mere proxy for class. The racial logic of this country is one that not only denies the full citizenship of Black people but also rejects their fundamental humanity. As a result, the Covid-19 pandemic has done more than demonstrate the absence of safety, health, and prosperity for Black people. It has also spotlighted the impossibility of such conditions within an empire built on unpaid African labor and justified through a process of racialization that stipulated that Black people were less moral, less intelligent, and, most significant, less human than White people.

Corona capitalism is built on neoliberal economic ideology, which views the free market as the answer to all our social problems. Austerity, efficiency, and privatization have become our "commonsense" responses to all our collective challenges. Private interests have become the stewards of the public good. This ideology allowed us to frame Covid-19 as an individual rather than collective problem. Washing our hands, taking our temperatures, and establishing social distance are framed as the only solutions to the pandemic, rather than also investing in communities, expanding the social safety net, and building sustainable institutions.

The United States is one of the richest countries in the world. But soon after the outbreak of the pandemic, the whole country was in crisis. Hospitals were overflowing; the frontline staff, nurses were using garbage bags as protection. How does "Corona capitalism" explain this happening in such a rich country?

Every aspect of our lives has been surrendered to the free market. This means that health care, both public and private, operates with the same profit-making logic as any other corporation.

Take New York, one of the hardest hit cities in the world, as an example. New York's hospital system has both public and private facilities. The public facilities, which serve the bulk of poor and working-class patients, are woefully under-funded. According to the Citizen's Budget Commission, the city's public and community hospitals operate with budget deficits as deep as $2.9 billion a year. The five large private networks, which serve a higher proportion of upper-mid-dle-class and wealthy patients, operate at a profit. These gaps in hospital funding have a direct impact on the quality of care that institutions can provide.

Given the shortcomings of our health insurance system, hospitals in underresourced areas are already stretched be-yond their intended role. On any given night, public hospi-tals in urban cities double as primary care facilities for the uninsured, homeless shelters, drug detox centers, and more. These same hospitals were then forced to treat a dispropor-tionate number of Covid-19 patients. This meant that people using the hospital for those unintended purposes were either pushed out, without alternative supports, or forced to linger in hospitals with high rates of infection and few resources to protect them. Since many of these people were already immunocompromised due to their preexisting health condi-tions, this became a matter of life and death.

The poorest hospitals were suddenly forced to manage all these issues with limited staff, space, and money. In many cities, hospital workers resorted to mixing their own hand sanitizer, reusing disposable masks for days at a time, and making their own PPE. While this is partly due to the fed-eral government's failure to properly prepare—for example, the national stockpile of protective face masks was only 30 million, well short of the 500 million to 1 billion recommended by some experts—this also reflects a larger structural problem. From schools to housing to food, our failure to invest in public institutions has placed the vulnerable and those who work with them at tremendous disadvantage. With regard to hospitals, our neglect of the public good has devastating consequences.

Of course, the financial impact of Covid-19 was not limited to the poorest hospitals. Wealthier hospitals also took huge economic hits as a result of the pandemic. Due to overcrowding and the threat of infection, they were unable to provide many medical services that were not related to Covid-19. Surgeries, cancer treatments, and other critical medical procedures couldn't be performed. This presented not only a medical challenge for those patients in need but a financial challenge for those hospitals that rely on such procedures for revenue.

Still, many private hospitals had enough resources to successfully withstand the lean financial months. Some facilities, like NYU Langone, were even able to take advantage of low interest rates and obtain hundreds of millions of dollars in credit. Such moves allowed these privileged institutions to remain financially secure in the short term and prepare for long-term growth and expansion. At the same time, poorer hospitals located in the most highly affected areas of the city were fighting for beds, ventilators, and PPE. So, once again, the economic elite were able to profit from disaster as the poor desperately fought for their lives. This reflects the perverse logic of Corona capitalism, in which healing is an industry and survival is a luxury.

But it wasn't just hospitals. The entire health care industry is implicated in this crisis.

Absolutely. We live in a country that does not value health care as a human right. Rather, we see it as yet another commodity. In the same way that we've tacitly accepted that poor people deserve poor education and poor housing, we have conceded that living on the economic margins means that you will not receive high-quality health care. The Covid-19 pandemic revealed how thoroughly dysfunctional and inhumane this system is.

In the United States, half of the country receives health care benefits through their employer. This meant that, during the height of the pandemic, millions lost not only their job but their access to health care. Many who held on to their coverage could not afford medicine, co-pays, and other associated costs. A poll by the Commonwealth Fund showed that 68 percent of Americans said that money would be a factor in their decision to seek care if they had coronavirus symptoms. The fact that people can die from a preventable or treatable illness simply because they do not have enough money proves how evil this system is.

And we cannot ignore the role of the pharmaceutical industry. Market logic pushes drug companies to prioritize

profit making over life saving. Instead of fully investing profits into research and development, many companies prefer
to wait until small companies make innovations, only to use
their vast resources to take control of the product. While this
is "good business," it does not maximize the possibility of
developing a life-saving drug.

During a pandemic, you might think these companies
would be more humane, right? Of course not. In April 2020,
Democrats in the US House of Representatives proposed
legislation designed to ensure that any effective Covid-19
drugs would be affordable and accessible to the entire country. Soon after, lobbying groups pushed back against the pro-
posal, arguing that price controls and other pro-consumer
measures were "dangerous, disruptive, and unacceptable."
These groups contended that they had the right to patent
and exclusively produce potentially life-saving drugs, even
during a pandemic—that these drugs were "American as-
sets." Sadly, this shameless appeal to the free market at a
moment in which more than 75,000 Americans had already
died is hardly surprising. In fact, it is business as usual.

*What about the US government. What do you make of its re-
sponse to the economic crisis?*

The government's response was wholly inadequate. Not
only did it fail to meet the needs of those most affected by
Covid-19, it only served to advance the interests of the very
institutions that created our current economic crisis.

In March 2020, Congress passed the CARES (Coronavirus Aid, Relief, and Economic Security) Act. This was a $2 trillion economic stimulus package, the largest in US history. As its name suggests, the legislation was sold to the public as a relief package for everyday people in the face of economic uncertainty. In reality, the bill did far more than that. Of that $2 trillion, $500 billion went to corporations in "distressed industries." Although Democrats fought for federal oversight of how the funds would be dispersed, Donald Trump made it clear that he would resist such regulation. The events after the economic recession of 2008, when corporate executives used bailout funds to pay themselves astronomical bonuses, revealed the waste, fraud, and abuse of these funds that we should expect. But even without this extra malfeasance, everyday people were forced to pay a 25 percent ransom to corporate America in order to receive economic relief.

The most trumpeted part of the CARES Act was the dispersal of money directly to taxpayers. Many individuals received a one-time $1,200 payment, which was actually a tax credit, in order to provide them with financial support. Unfortunately, disorganization and logistical challenges made it difficult for people to access the funds. For example, many people without access to a formal lending institution or electronic banking had to wait months to receive their checks. These were often the same people who needed those funds the most. Most important, $1,200 was woefully inadequate for providing meaningful help to people who were unable to earn money for months, maybe longer.

What about small businesses?

Small businesses were also supposed to be targeted through the Paycheck Protection Program (PPP). The PPP program was authorized through the CARES Act to provide $349 billion in low-interest loans of up to $10 million to companies with fewer than 500 employees. These loans were intended to provide an emergency cash injection to small businesses so that they could continue to pay employees, as well as other regular monthly expenses. Given the vulnerability of small businesses during the pandemic, this was an important and necessary provision. In practice, however, many small businesses were also subordinated to the interests of corporate America.

Many of the companies accessing PPP loans hardly met the standard of a "small business." In April 2020, the Associated Press revealed that $365 million of the funds had been given to ninety-four publicly traded companies. Twenty-five percent of these companies had indicated to investors that they were facing financial insolvency months before the Covid-19 crisis. The AP also reported that $273 million of early funds went to one hundred companies that were owned or operated by people who had donated at least $11.1 million since May 2015 to Donald Trump's campaign, the Republican National Committee, or America First Action, a Trump-endorsed super political action committee.

Successful companies like Chembio Diagnostics, a multinational company that produces infectious disease tests, received $10 million, despite the fact that its stock doubled after it was approved to produce a rapid Covid-19 test. Rather than saving a struggling business, these funds were used to help a successful company become more successful. This was not an unusual example. Legal loopholes allowed companies with thousands of employees to apply for loans based on the number of employees at individual locations. This is how Shake Shack, a fast-food chain worth $2.8 billion that employs more than 6,000 people, was able to secure $10 million dollars in small business funds (though, after this was revealed, the company was pressured to return the loan). These examples spotlight how Corona capitalism normalizes an environment where the poor are stigmatized for having legitimate need while corporations are the undeserving beneficiary of a generous welfare system.

What about individual wealth?

It is difficult to disentangle corporate wealth from individual wealth, as the country's wealthiest people are tied to some of the country's richest and most powerful companies. How do we separate Elon Musk from Tesla, Eric Yuan from Zoom, or Jeff Bezos from Amazon?

In early April 2020, the same month in which 20 million Americans had filed for unemployment, US billionaires' wealth grew by nearly 10 percent, passing $3.2 trillion. As of June, when 42.6 million had filed for unemployment over the previous eleven weeks, US billionaires were 20 percent richer, adding $565 billion to their collective wealth.

These numbers show the inherent immorality of a system that produces billionaires to begin with. It is literally impossible to amass such gross amounts of money without being directly connected to various forms of human suffering. No amount of philanthropy, activism, or principled reinvestment can change that.

You mentioned Jeff Bezos, the CEO and founder of Amazon. No individual or company has financially benefited more from the Covid-19 pandemic. How do you make sense of this?

With a personal net worth of more than $200 billion, Bezos is the richest human being in modern history. In the first quarter of 2020, against the backdrop of global pandemic, his personal net worth increased by nearly $24 billion. Beyond being a primary player in the current crisis, Bezos and Amazon are the poster children for Corona capitalism.

Prior to the pandemic, Amazon built a historically unprecedented economic empire by avoiding taxes, exploiting workers, and dominating markets in ways that starve and ultimately kill small businesses. Amazon began its empire by using what is referred to as a "beachhead strategy," or dominating a small market area and then using it as a stronghold from which to expand into other products and markets. Bezos started by taking over the online book market, selling books at prices with which no brick-and-mortar store could compete. The success of Amazon caused the shutdown not only of major bookseller chains but also independent bookstores around the country. For Amazon, profits weren't the primary goal. Rather, it was knocking out all competition and controlling as much of the market as possible. Twenty-five years later, Amazon has succeeded. The company is the second largest private employer in the United States and, by 2021, will account for 50 percent of all online sales nationwide.

With this control comes extraordinary power. Amazon has the political power to shape local and federal policy, determine labor standards, and shield itself from democratic accountability. Despite having earned billions in profits, Amazon pays very little in taxes. In 2019, Amazon reported $280 billion in total revenue and $13.9 billion in pre-tax income. Still, according to the US Securities and Exchange Commission, the company only had to pay $162 million in taxes. Although the federal corporate tax rate is 21 percent, tax loopholes allowed Amazon to only pay 1.2 percent. Sadly, this was progress from 2018, when it paid zero dollars in taxes, and 2017, when it received a $137 million refund.

At the same time that Amazon is earning historically unprecedented amounts of cash, the company's workers have continued to suffer. Low wages and unhealthy working conditions have been central to Amazon's business model of "consumer friendliness." While Amazon earns tax breaks by accepting SNAP (Supplemental Nutrition Assistance Program) subsidies from customers, its employees are among the top food stamp recipients in numerous states around the country. Again, this was true *before* the Covid-19 pandemic.

Once the country began to shut down, Amazon quickly became the only game in town. With so many people stuck at home, Amazon became the only way for many to access necessary goods. And with a severely shrunken labor market, Amazon was the only available employment for many workers. Essentially, twenty-five years of predatory business practices put it in a position to exploit an unforeseeable human crisis. This is the essence of Corona capitalism.

Supporters of capitalism will say that Amazon's success is just a natural function of the free market. How do you respond to that?

There is nothing natural or free about capitalism. Companies like Amazon become economic behemoths because of government policies that allow them to be so. They are rescued from the "natural" effects of the market when institutions like the Federal Deposit Insurance Corporation and Federal Reserve decide that they are "too big to fail." While the right rails against the threat of socialism, they actively support government interventions that ensure that the wealthy benefit.

Within the rules and logic of this system, Amazon did nothing wrong. The company simply responded to the demands of the system. The problem, however, is that the system is engineered to ensure that certain people are winners and losers. Imagine playing a competitive sport where one of the competitors also gets to create the rules, design the playing field, and be one of the referees. This is precisely what happens within Corona capitalism.

Think about the people who were caught selling hand sanitizer, masks, and other protective items at exorbitant prices. In some instances, people were selling hand sanitizer for four hundred dollars a case. The corporate media quickly exposed these individuals, while the Department of Justice and Federal Bureau of Investigation threatened to bring the full force of the law to punish them. And Amazon, with no sense of irony, went to Congress and demanded legislation against price gouging. The hypocrisy is stunning.

Focusing on individual price gouging seems like such a small drop in the bucket.

It is. Obviously, I don't support price gouging. During a moment of crisis, we should be looking to support and protect, not prey on, each other. Still, economic desperation produces these kinds of decisions. Also, the culture of capitalism teaches us to think in market terms. We are taught to focus on our "brands" rather than our reputations. We are taught to view citizenship through the lens of consumership rather than democratic participation. We are taught to view each other as means rather than ends. Within this framework, it is no surprise that people would view the pandemic through the lens of market demand.

But it's pointless to focus on the few everyday people who exploited the crisis. They are symptoms of the larger crisis of Corona capitalism. The person selling hand sanitizer for four hundred dollars doesn't have the power to normalize their exploitative practices. This is why a desperate citizen making thousands from Covid-19 masks creates a moral panic, while transnational corporations making billions from the same pandemic is accepted as the proper functioning of the "free" market.

The issue of power is key here. Due to its massive economic influence, Amazon has the ability to regulate consumer practices, shape public policy, and control global markets. The emergence of Corona capitalism has only expedited the consolidation of privatized power. Corporations, not governments, are the primary shapers of our lives. As a result, we are shedding even the pretense of political transparency, democratic practices, social safety nets, or a fundamental investment in the lives of the vulnerable.

And this type of exploitation is not particular to the Covid-19 pandemic, right?

Definitely not. As Naomi Klein describes in her brilliant book *The Shock Doctrine*, natural disasters and human crises are prime sites of opportunity for predatory forms of capitalism. Whenever the masses are in a state of shock and disorientation caused by a crisis, the powerful intervene with ostensible solutions that expand their wealth and widen the gap between the have-gots and the have-nots. The rise of private military contractors and "tax-free enterprise zones" for corporations in New Orleans after Hurricane Katrina, the emergence of private security companies after the September 11 attacks, the infiltration of Western oil companies into Iraqi oil fields after the Iraq War, and the massive corporate bailouts during the 2008 financial crisis are examples of how unexpected crises become the pretext for developing policies and institutional arrangements that have longstanding impacts on the economy, environment, law, and everyday life.

In the current moment of Corona capitalism, we are witnessing an even more naked and aggressive articulation of Klein's thesis. Through the shock of an unprecedented global health crisis, government and corporate elites are quickly threatening to implement long-held goals. In a few short months, the Trump administration has used the discourse of "national emergency" as an excuse to impose a lethal southern border security policy, undermine unions, and privatize school lunch programs. The fossil fuel industry has used the pandemic to garner financial benefit and justify various forms of deregulation. These are just a few examples of how the powerful are radically reshaping the world as many of us remain in a state of shock, work to navigate the challenges of everyday life, and actively resist the current structures of power.

DEATH-ELIGIBLE

There has been very little conversation about the impact of Covid-19 within prisons. Why do you think that is?

The lack of conversation about the impact of Covid-19 on incarcerated populations is disturbing but hardly surprising. Although there is a growing conversation about the crisis of incarceration in this country, we still fail to view those living inside of prisons as full human beings, much less full citizens. In moments of crisis, even ones where we attempt to universalize our pain, prison populations are easily forgotten. With more than 2.2 million people currently caged inside of US prisons and jails, this is not only an irresponsible oversight but the foundation of a political, moral, and public health crisis.

In May 2020, the Federal Bureau of Prisons reported that 70 percent of the incarcerated people who were tested for Covid-19 had positive results. By June, there were more than 42,000 reported Covid-19 infections and 510 deaths. The infection rate within US prisons had become five and a half times higher than the general population. In other words, these are death camps.

The increased likelihood of Covid-19 death within prison is attributable to several factors. Like the rest of the country, US prisons did not have sufficient testing equipment, which made it difficult to determine how many prisoners and staff were infected. This resource gap was compounded by the government's failure to accurately count the number of positive cases that it did find. For example, in May 2020, the Centers for Disease Control and Prevention (CDC) reported that nearly 5,000 prisoners had tested positive for coronavirus. Two weeks later, Reuters documented more than 17,000 cases within local, state, and federal facilities. Such gross discrepancies made it difficult to properly track the pandemic or produce an appropriate response.

In the peak of the pandemic in New York, no place on Earth was more infectious than the Rikers Island jail complex. As of July 2020, infection rates were 7.86 percent, as compared to 2.62 percent in New York City and 0.81 percent throughout the entire United States. How do we arrive at such astronomically high numbers without an outcry from the public or an urgent response from the government?

Of course, no one deserves to die from Covid-19. But it is worth noting that 75 percent of the people incarcerated in Rikers have not been convicted of a crime. Most of them are awaiting trial and remain in prison because they cannot afford cash bail. Since the US legal system allegedly deems everyone "innocent until proven guilty," this means that there are countless innocent people dying in prison simply because they do not have enough money to live. Covid-19 has turned their ordinary criminal cases into death sentences without benefit of trial, judge, or jury.

The burden of poverty also shows up in the prison health-care system. In prisons around the country, incarcerated people are charged medical co-pays in order to schedule a doctor's visit, receive dental care, or access medicine. These co-pays can range from two to five dollars per visit. Since most incarcerated people earn little or no money—the average non-industry prison worker earns between fourteen and sixty-three cents an hour—these co-pays are unconscionably high. In some states, a prisoner can spend an entire week's pay just to visit a doctor. Like in the outside world, these high co-pays discourage people from seeking medical attention until their health condition becomes more serious or, at times, irreversible.

Another factor within prisons is the lack of PPE. Masks, gloves, and other materials are rarely distributed within many of the nation's prisons. Adding insult to injury, many incarcerated people have been asked to produce these very materials while being denied access to them. For example, governor Andrew Cuomo responded to state-wide shortages in New York by making state prisoners sew masks and bottle hand sanitizer. Imagine the cruel irony of being asked to risk your life in a crowded and unsafe work area, for less than a dollar a day, to make materials that you might not be able to use.

Social distancing is a primary way of preventing infection. But how can one consistently remain six feet apart from others within a prison? Many prison cells are overcrowded, leaving people with literally no room to safely distance from others. In most prisons, it is not uncommon for beds to be only a few feet apart. Lines for food, phone calls, and showers often do not allow for adequate social distancing. Prison guards can also contribute to the spread of coronavirus, as many are untested and asymptomatic. They interact with the outside world every day and can bring the virus into the prison and spread it across various parts of the building without knowing it.

Many prisons have responded to the threat of coronavirus through repressive tactics. Rather than investing in resources that create safer and healthier conditions for everyone, prison officials in many states have intensified the use of solitary confinement, also known as "restrictive" or "segregated" housing. Regardless of the name, the practice is the same: social isolation and deprivation, as well as the denial of recreation, exercise, or any form of communication with the outside world. Medical doctors, psychologists, prison scholars, and international bodies like the United Nations have stated that solitary confinement is a form of torture that should be eliminated. Still, before Covid-19, there were sixty thousand people in solitary confinement in US state and federal prisons. After the pandemic, that number skyrocketed to three hundred thousand.

Consider what this means for the incarcerated. For many, their fate is either to die slowly from the torture of solitary confinement or die quickly from exposure to Covid-19. The absurdity of these options reflects the cruelty of our criminal justice system and our gross indifference to the well-being of those caged inside of US prisons. But it's not just prisoners who have been ignored. We must also look to other spaces of confinement within the United States, from nursing homes to immigrant detention centers, which became even more dangerous, dehumanizing, and deadly during the pandemic.

Why is it important for us to think about confinement as a concept?

Because confinement is a quintessentially American practice and a centerpiece of American life. At every juncture in history, the practice of human confinement has been used to expand empire, justify the dehumanization and exploitation of vulnerable populations, and hide the ugliest blemishes of what bell hooks aptly refers to as a White supremacist, patriarchal, capitalist empire.

Confinement reflects the conditions under which so many vulnerable people have lived within the United States. The enslavement of African people is the inaugural practice of the nation-state. Mass incarceration is another state-sanctioned form of captivity that prevents the exercise of Black freedom. The "ghetto" was constructed to contain those ethnic groups that lacked access to American Whiteness. The home has historically been a space of confinement for women, marking the boundaries of their labor and naturalizing male domination. The metaphor of "the closet" signals the physical and discursive limits of legitimate identity and performance for those queer folk trapped inside of it.

Confinement not only restricts human freedom but also denies the fundamental humanity of those being confined. The practice of confinement has become increasingly prevalent as the country further embraces what critical theorist Henry Giroux calls the "politics of disposability." More than ever before, human confinement has become a normalized condition of the American social contract.

What is the politics of disposability?

The politics of disposability is part and parcel of the current neoliberal moment. The logic of the market shapes every aspect of our lives. Our values, our political choices, our social interactions, and our cultural practices are all bound up in the logic of profit making. The language of competition and efficiency has come to color nearly every dimension of our lives. The public good has been trumped by the private interest. Individual success, rather than collective well-being, is understood as the definition of social progress.

Within this neoliberal universe, citizenship is measured by our ability to be consumers. Individuals are only as valuable as their ability to produce and consume. The most vulnerable populations, those who need the most from our social safety net, are viewed as burdens unworthy of investment, protection, or care. Since they have no value to us in terms of market logic, we express no collective concern for them. We do not care whether they live or die. They are disposable.

In the United States, there has always been a relationship between disposability and confinement. Our willingness to consign people to spaces of confinement is directly related to our assessment of their economic value. This assessment is informed by the logics of White supremacy, patriarchy, and capitalism.

Confinement has long been used as a way of meeting the needs of the capitalist market. Think about how mass incarceration emerged in the aftermath of legal slavery. After emancipation, Black people were no longer the private property of White slaveowners. This rendered them less valuable with regard to the Southern economy. Since the Thirteenth Amendment outlawed human slavery except for punishment of a crime, the government ensured that everything Black people did became a crime. The creation of the Black Codes led to the widespread criminalization of Black people, which led to their confinement within jails and prisons. Through the convict-lease system, Black prisoners were leased to private businesses like railroad companies, coal mines, and sometimes the very same plantations from which they had been emancipated.

The practice of lynching, as a widespread form of racial terrorism and extrajudicial violence, did not begin until the end of slavery. This is not a coincidence. When Black people were the legal property of White men, there was no desire to kill them. Slave masters would prefer to sell them or, if necessary, have the court system impose punishment. That way, they could be legally compensated for their losses. After all, Black people were property. Why would they destroy something from which they generated wealth? It was only after the end of slavery, when our captivity was no longer directly linked to profit making, that Black lives were so easily disposable. This is a quintessentially American logic: the moment you are no longer exploitable, you become death-eligible.

In the current neoliberal moment, the politics of disposability has become the dominant order of the day. Over the past four decades, we have responded to so many of our social crises by "throwing away" the people suffering from them. Consider, for example, how we have come to treat mental illness. In 1980, President Jimmy Carter signed the Mental Health Systems Act. This legislation was designed to increase and expand resources for people with mental illnesses. The following year, President Ronald Reagan repealed the act, beginning decades of federal divestment from mental health resources. This placed many people with mental illness on the street, left to fend for themselves. At the same time, we passed numerous state and local laws that criminalized living on the street. Prisons were increasingly filled with people dealing with untreated mental illnesses.

By essentially criminalizing people with mental illness, we demonstrated our investment in their disposability. We've done this with so many other social challenges, like poverty, drug addiction, and homelessness. We have committed to resolving our contradictions by hiding, erasing, and confining people. And if they perish, they perish.

This politics of disposability follows an economic logic. But how are people convinced to accept it?

Confinement and disposability are shaped by economic logics, but they are also reflected in our social beliefs and cultural practices. They become part of the everyday, taken-for-granted ways that we navigate the world.

The United States has 2.2 million people living inside jails and prisons, a number unprecedented in human history. We allow this to happen by convincing ourselves that there is a criminal class of people, a group that deserves the fate of incarceration. We convince ourselves that no one in these prisons is wrongfully accused. We ignore the fact that the average person commits multiple crimes every day—as Harvey Silverglate describes in his book *Three Felonies a Day*—and decide that anyone in prison is a bad person. And where do we put bad people? Prison. It becomes a circular logic.

And think about how often we've heard jokes about "not dropping the soap" in prison. The fact that these jokes occur within mainstream conversations and popular culture speaks to the pervasiveness of rape culture, which normalizes and justifies various forms of sexual violence, as well as homophobia. But it also shows how the politics of disposability determines that those living in confinement deserve whatever fate happens to them.

I would also push back against the idea that the politics of disposability is purely a reflection of economic logic. Consider, for example, the role of heteropatriarchy in normalizing domestic violence and sexual assault against women. As Black feminist scholars have noted, issues of intimate partner violence have historically been considered a private rather than public concern. This is due to the belief that women are the property of their male partners and therefore shielded from public accountability. In this regard, the home is not only a space of confinement but a site of what Angela Davis calls "the privatized punishment of women."

Covid-19 is just another reminder of the extraordinary sense of disposability that we assign to those who are in spaces of confinement.

In addition to prisons, what were some other spaces of confinement whose vulnerabilities were exposed during the Covid-19 pandemic?

Well, let's continue with the domestic sphere, which is one of the most ignored spaces of confinement. For many women around the globe, the home remains a site of containment and violence. Through legal mandates, cultural norms, and economic realities, many women are formally or informally confined to their homes. Within these spaces, intimate partner violence and sexual assault remain the norm. According to UN Women, 243 million women and girls reported that they had been subjected to physical and sexual violence by an intimate partner between 2019 and 2020. These conditions were only exacerbated by the pandemic.

Experts say that domestic violence increases when people face economic pressure, lose their jobs, or experience moments of crisis. For many households, Covid-19 produced all three factors, while also eliminating opportunities for escape. Women, girls, and femmes who could normally escape violent situations at least temporarily by going outside, visiting family and friends, or going to work were now confined to their homes with their abusers. One month into the pandemic, domestic violence hotlines around the world reported an increase in calls. Those areas that did not report an increase may signal an even graver danger, as many women no longer have the physical space or adequate conditions to seek help.

Home confinement created other problems for child-bearing people. In April 2020, the United Nations Population Fund predicted that 44 million women in 114 low and middle-income countries could lose access to contraception, leading to 1 million unwanted pregnancies during a three-month lockdown or 7 million for a six-month lockdown. In addition, they predicted the possibility of an additional 13 million child marriages and 2 million cases of female genital mutilation, as the pandemic undermined efforts at stopping both.

These examples are reminders of the gendered blind spots of our Covid-19 analysis. While the home is typically constructed as a safe space and refuge from danger, it remains the opposite for many women, girls, and femmes. Too often, however, we still think about the violence that occurs inside of homes as a private rather than public matter. We also continue to decenter the experiences of anyone who is not gendered male.

You mentioned nursing homes earlier. Where do the elderly fit into this politics of disposability?

The pandemic has had a devastating impact on the elderly. As of June 2020, nearly 40 percent of all Covid-19 deaths occurred in long-term care facilities. This includes nursing homes, hospices, and residential care facilities. This stands to reason, as nursing homes are overwhelmingly populated by the elderly, for whom it is a greater challenge to fight coronavirus than it is for their younger counterparts. Still, it would be a mistake to dismiss the death rates of the elderly within these spaces as a mere "natural" occurrence.

Like prisons, nursing homes are institutions where death is normalized. When a prisoner dies, we view it as an unfortunate but acceptable consequence of someone who made bad choices. When someone in a nursing home passes, we view it as a sad but "natural" part of life. Of course, death is indeed a natural and inevitable part of the human experience. But too often, we consign the elderly to death even when it is entirely avoidable. For example, four hundred thousand nursing home residents die every year from infections. Many of these deaths are preventable when nursing home staff are performing their jobs with the proper care and consistency. Unfortunately, this is often not the case. Between 2017 and 2020, 75 percent of US nursing homes were cited for failing to properly monitor and control infections.

It would be too simplistic, however, to attribute the death of the elderly to simple human cruelty. The failure of nursing homes to protect the elderly is a reflection of the neoliberal system that produces them. More than 70 percent of the nursing home industry operates on a for-profit basis. This means economic efficiency becomes more important than health. As a result, overcrowded facilities, underpaid staff, and low-quality care are common features of nursing homes. These conditions only worsened after Covid-19.

The pandemic placed considerable pressure on nursing homes to protect their extremely vulnerable elderly population. Still, despite the clear need to hire more staff, institute new procedures, and purchase more equipment, many nursing homes were reluctant to implement changes that would compromise their profit margins. Many nursing home staff are low-wage employees who are forced to work multiple jobs in order to piece together a living. This increases their own health vulnerability as well as the risks to the patients they serve.

And our disregard for the elderly isn't exclusive to nursing homes. At every turn during the pandemic, political calculations were made that conceded the disposability of the elderly. At the beginning of the pandemic, when ventilators and hospital beds were in short supply, it quickly became "common sense" that age should be a deciding factor for who received them. In New York and New Jersey, policies were created that demanded that nursing homes accept all patients, regardless of their Covid-19 status. These mandates also prohibited the testing of potential new residents. These decisions cleared hospital space for younger and healthier people, while placing the elderly at a heightened risk.

Our willingness to sacrifice the elderly became most clear in the public debates about ending the shutdowns. President Trump, in his initial desire to reopen the country by Easter, ignored the extraordinary risk that such a move would make for highly vulnerable elderly populations. But Trump was not alone. The most clear and unabashed example of this perspective came from Texas lieutenant governor Dan Patrick, who argued that people over seventy years old should be willing to risk their lives as a "sacrifice" to prevent "ruining America" through economic collapse. Patrick said the elderly should endorse reopening the country, even though it meant greatly increasing their chances of dying, in order to protect US economic interests. Such attitudes reflect the belief that the decision of who lives or dies should be determined through market logic. Based on this ideology, the elderly have the least to contribute and are the most disposable.

Of course, there are economic counterarguments to this position. Americans over fifty years old make up 35 percent of the population, 40 percent of the gross domestic product, and 43 percent of the tax base. There is a strong case to be made that high death rates among the elderly would compromise the stability of the economy. But to appeal to such arguments is to lend legitimacy to a gross necropolitical calculation. Instead, we must critically interrogate the current system: Why do we have such little regard for the elderly? How do we ethically determine who gets to live or die? What does it mean for us to prioritize profit making over life saving?

Until we confront these questions, and seriously imagine new possibilities, we will continue to live in a state of disposability.

THE SPECTACLE OF VIOLENCE

In recent years, video footage has been instrumental in the fight against police brutality and other forms of racism. Why has this been the case?

Over the past decade, advanced video, photo, and audio technologies have become increasingly easy to obtain. This is largely due to the emergence of cell phones as a central part of everyday life. According to a 2015 Pew poll, more than 90 percent of Americans own a cell phone and nearly 70 percent have a smartphone. Among youth ages eighteen to twenty-nine, smartphone ownership is more than 85 percent. Second, the expansion of smartphone-centered technologies has allowed for high-resolution photography, video recording, and live broadcasting. These tools enable everyday people to engage in what I refer to in my research as "new surveillances," or a reshaping of the relationships of surveillance between individuals and the state.

Since Black people were brought to the Americas, we have

been the subjects of state-sponsored and state-sanctioned surveillance. From slavery-era flesh branding to COINTEL-PRO-era phone tapping, various technologies have been used to monitor, control, discipline, and punish Black folk. Since 9/11, these forms of surveillance have not only continued but have been codified into law under the guise of economic efficiency, public safety, and national security.

These new surveillances have created greater space for resistance. In the current moment, everyday citizens can pull out a cell phone to record an act of police violence and photograph the inhumane conditions of a prison. These technologies allow us to produce tangible and legible evidence of the various forms of violence experienced by Black people in the United States.

Why is the emergence of video technology particularly significant for Black people?

Because Black witness has always been insufficient. Whether in a court of law or everyday life, the idea of Black people being credible observers has never been accepted. This is partly due to longstanding White supremacist questions about our character ("Are they telling the truth about what happened?"), our intelligence ("Are they capable of properly assessing what happened?"), and our fundamental worth ("Do we care even if something did happen?"), which have made attempts to articulate our experiences both unpersuasive and uncompelling.

The other issue is denial. American culture is committed to nostalgia, erasure, and outright dishonesty as its response to trauma. Instead of reckoning with our violent history of conquest and plunder, we tell romantic stories of brave and principled European explorers. Rather than viewing slavery as a foundational component of the country, with ongoing impacts in every sector of our lives, we dismiss it as a brief and morally troublesome interruption to an otherwise principled and longstanding journey toward democracy. We ignore painful truths as a strategy for maintaining national pride and justifying acts of evil.

For White Americans, the denial of racism allows them to justify their unearned power. It also enables them to justify doing nothing to disrupt the systems that privilege them. When White people are forced to view spectacles of violence against Black people, they are forced to bear witness to truths that they previously denied. They must then reconcile these truths with their previously held beliefs, understandings, and claims about the world.

So why hasn't the recent wave of video footage led to more arrests and convictions, or at least more national outrage?

I believe that it has. The killing of Ahmaud Arbery, the unarmed Black male jogger killed by Travis McMichael with the help of his father, Gregory McMichael, was one of the most brutal instances of violence that we've seen in recent years. Even the people who attempted to posthumously depict Ar-

bery as a criminal generally conceded that his death was unnecessary. There was nearly universal outrage at the killing of
George Floyd at the hands of Derek Chauvin, the police officer who kept his knee on Floyd's neck for eight minutes and
forty-six seconds. Even media outlets like Fox News, which
ritually excuse police brutality and criminalize Black victims
of state violence, conceded that Chauvin's behavior was wrong.

Video footage has done more than just sway public sen-
timent. The firing of the four police officers associated with
Floyd's death only occurred because of video footage, which
not only captured brutal details but also contradicted police
claims that he had resisted arrest. Arbery was killed in February 2020, but there was no movement on the case until
the video footage was released to the public in May. Even
when the state is not invested in justice, video footage can
force its hand.

Still, we must be careful not to overestimate the power
of video footage. Even in the face of video evidence, many
White people struggle to accept new findings. For example, in
1991, the entire country watched a videotape of Rodney King,
an unarmed Black man, being kicked and beaten by four Los
Angeles police officers for fifteen minutes. When the King
tape was released and broadcast widely, many White people
expressed shock and outrage that the incident had occurred.
Still, the following year, a nearly all-White jury acquitted all
four officers of assault and three of the four of excessive force.

In the face of hard video evidence, how could the jury
not find the officers guilty? Ultimately, they were persuaded

by the defense's argument, which was that King was a "PCP-crazed giant." The jurors were convinced by the argument that brutally beating King was the only way to stop him from harming the officers and other innocent people throughout the city. In essence, the jury ignored what they saw in order to justify a clear and egregious case of police brutality.

How could this happen? What must one have to believe about King to accept such an argument? In this case, the jury accepted arguments about King as being evil and prone to violence. They also accepted the claim that he was not capable of experiencing pain in the same way as "normal" people. Such beliefs were informed by deeply rooted White supremacist narratives about Black immorality, as well as the belief that our inhuman status renders us impervious to pain. Rather than accepting what they could plainly see, a Black man mercilessly beaten by police, they chose to cling to wildly irrational White supremacist logic.

This is why we cannot fetishize the power of video. We cannot convince ourselves that "hard proof" was the missing link in the struggle against racialized state violence. To do so would be to let White people off the hook for their active and intentional investments in White supremacy.

Of course, many White people would do better if they knew better. But it would be naïve to believe that White people have not dismantled the current system simply because they were unaware of it, or even because they were untrusting of Black witness. We have to be honest about the fact that White ignorance is often *willful*. It is easier to embrace

racist myths than to admit that one's privilege is unearned.
It is more convenient to ignore compelling evidence than to
concede unjust power.

This is why, even after watching Walter Scott get shot in
the back in 2015 by officer Michael Slager in North Charles-
ton, South Carolina, as Scott ran away from him, the first jury
could not reach a unanimous guilty verdict. This is how the
entire world witnessed Eric Garner being choked to death by
Daniel Pantaleo on Staten Island, yet the officer was never
indicted. For many White Americans, it is better to accept a
comforting lie than an unsettling truth. To accept that Black
people are routinely terrorized by the state would force them
to confront their most coveted beliefs about the country. To
concede that Black people are treated as subhuman because
they are not White would force them to forge new moral, eth-
ical, psychological, and political commitments. If they aren't
prepared to do this, then it will never happen.

This doesn't mean that video footage isn't valuable. Many
people have radically altered their beliefs and actions after
being forced to reckon with some of these images. In practical terms, the mobilization of video has been one of the only
tactics that has produced accountability for harm done to
Black people. Still, if someone is committed to worshipping
a lie, the truth cannot convert them.

Have you seen the actual video of George Floyd's death?

Yes, but I didn't want to.

Why not?

It was a question of self-care. I have to protect my own emotional and psychological well-being. As an activist and scholar of state violence, I knew that I would eventually watch it. But after hearing the brutal details of Floyd's death, I wasn't prepared to view the actual footage.

Years of watching Black people die, both in my personal life and my professional work, have taken a severe toll on me. I have to prepare myself. Unfortunately, I was not given the opportunity. As I scrolled through social media, I was assaulted by numerous videos and photos that showed every second of Derek Chauvin brutally killing George Floyd. No preparation. No warning. It left me shaken.

And this was not an isolated incident. Every day, we are bombarded by the spectacle of violence. Television, film, music, billboards, videogames, social media, and traditional media all confront us with extraordinary levels of violence. This violence takes many forms, but anti-Black violence is near the top of the list. From Eric Garner to Ahmaud Arbery to George Floyd, we are constantly forced to witness the brutal killings of Black people, both by the state and citizens.

So there's a danger in showing these images so frequently?

Absolutely, but it is also quite complicated. Given the denial of Black people's experiences with racism and state violence, these images can be quite valuable. Black people now have unprecedented access to visual testimonies, which corroborate the stories we have been telling for centuries. The proliferation of images can be powerful because they resonate with our own experiences and help articulate our pain.

At the same time, and for many of the same reasons that they are valuable, these images are also deeply harmful. Given the ordinariness of racialized violence in the lives of Black people, both from the state and ordinary citizens, the constant exposure to images of anti-Black violence can be triggering for many of us. Every time we turn on the news or log on to our social media accounts, we are forced to reengage some of our most traumatic individual and collective experiences. No other group of people in America has to routinely deal with that.

We must also consider how the constant representation of violence against Black people can undermine collective outrage. We already live in world where Black death is normalized. Our vulnerability doesn't provoke the same sympathy, outrage, or political response as that of our White counterparts. When there is a school shooting in a White suburb, the public says things like, "This shouldn't happen here." This corresponds with the dominant belief that White suburbs, White schools, and White lives are entitled to uninterrupted peace and safety. The unspoken corollary to this belief is that such tragedies can be reasonably expected to occur elsewhere. And, of course, "elsewhere" is wherever those on the bottom of the social ladder dwell.

This is why, when we hear media stories about famine in Africa or shootings in Chicago, so many people are unmoved.

It's not that people *want* death to occur in these places, but that they have come to "naturally" associate these places with disaster, misfortune, violence, and premature death. This is because we only hear media stories about the continent of Africa in relation to violence and poverty. Mainstream media discourse has made Chicago shorthand for tribalized violence and political corruption. As a result, events that correlate with these storylines do not upset us. This is the same for images of anti-Black violence. The more we see it, the easier it is to be unbothered by it.

In the aftermath of the Rodney King trial, many experts argued that the constant repetition of the beating desensitized the jury to its brutality. They suggested that they saw King's body beaten so frequently that the event was stripped of its brutality. They no longer saw King as a human being with whom they could empathize, but as a text available for close reading.

In the era of twenty-four-hour cable news and social media, a similar desensitization happens to all of us. When we are repeatedly forced to view Black people being beaten, tortured, and killed, it becomes harder to sustain our outrage. How many times can we watch Ahmaud Arbery getting shot down like an animal before we begin to objectify his body? How does witnessing the repetition of inhumane treatment against Black people reinforce the White supremacist belief that we are indeed not human? These questions aren't just abstract or academic. They have a real impact on how we navigate the world.

Every time that Black people are forced to witness systematic violence against people who look like us, and those whom we love, we are taught about our lack of value within this country. We are sent a message that unmerited suffering is an inevitable part of Black life. We are reminded of the precarity of our own lives. This does profound damage to our spirits, our psyches, our culture, and our politics.

Derek Chauvin stayed with his knee on Floyd's neck for four minutes after Floyd had lost consciousness. A firefighter who watched as this unfolded said to Chauvin, "Check his pulse." Still, Chauvin kept his knee on Floyd's neck for four minutes while Floyd was already unconscious. Is the dehumanization so profound that for Chauvin it is like killing an animal?

The specifics of this case are complicated because there are many unresolved questions about Chauvin's background, whether he knew George Floyd from a job they previously shared, and whether or not his actions were the product of personal animus. What we know for certain is that Chauvin's behavior, with his knee on that man's neck for eight minutes and forty-six seconds, is a common police practice.

As I mentioned before, this indifference to Black people's lives is not only indebted to the racist hatred of Black people, but also the White supremacist narrative that Black people are impervious to normal human pain because we are not actually human. But we also do not want to let the perpetrators of violence off the hook. We cannot pretend that White violence is merely a product of bad information or lack of information. We cannot ignore the fact that Derek Chauvin showed a vicious indifference to George Floyd's suffering. Chauvin did not care about Floyd's painful screams, his desperate cries for his mother, his repeated assertion that he could not breathe, or his dreadful declaration that he was going to die. And although Chauvin was the only person with his knee on Floyd's neck, we cannot ignore the fact that there were three other officers standing there, watching this happen. They were all complicit in this spectacle of violence.

You've used the word spectacle *a few times. Why is it important to think of these incidents as spectacles?*

I use the term *spectacle* to draw attention to the role of visuality in how we come to understand incidents of violence. Our individual and collective response to these incidents is directly connected to our ability to see, and in many cases hear, what has transpired. The current technological moment enables us to record and distribute these incidents in ways that allow global communities of people to bear witness.

The spectacle of violence is also about the public nature of these events. When the state inflicts violence in full public view, the impact reaches beyond just the person who suffers the violence. As the philosopher Michel Foucault argued in *Discipline and Punish*, public forms of state violence also have a profound impact on those who bear witness to it. Within the American context, we must also look at how this plays out along racial lines.

Think about the practice of lynching in the United States. Lynchings were not only executions but social events. White southerners ate lunch and drank whiskey as Black bodies dangled from trees in front of them. The severed fingers, toes, and genitalia of murdered Blacks were taken as physical keepsakes of the festivities. Postcards with images of the lynchings were routinely sent through the mail. White lynch mobs did not just kill Black people, they turned them into public spectacles that reinforced White supremacy.

The lynching was not only a sadistic and illegal form of punishment but also a form of racial terrorism. The public torture, killing, and desecration of Black bodies sent a clear message about the practical consequences of disrupting or even questioning the system of racial hierarchy. The spectacle of violence was used as a perpetual reminder that the institutions of American democracy—the law, the court system, the prisons, the police—were incapable of protecting Black people from White supremacist fear, rage, and violence.

Today, we continue to witness the public executions of Black people through extrajudicial means. Police officers like Darren Wilson and Derek Chauvin, as well as private citizens like George Zimmerman and Travis McMichael, continue to operate as the judge, jury, and executioner of Black people like Michael Brown, Renisha McBride, George Floyd, Rekia Boyd, Trayvon Martin, Breonna Taylor, and Ahmaud Arbery.

When Michael Brown was killed by officer Darren Wilson in Ferguson, Missouri, his body lay on the ground for four and a half hours. As I write in my book *Nobody*, the spectacle of his death not only sent a chilling message to the local community, but its mass distribution and consumption on social media transformed it into a global event.

Digital technologies have made the audience for such events even broader and the circulation of them much faster. Now, every time we watch the news or log on to Facebook, Instagram, TikTok, or Twitter, we become audience to the spectacle of Black death, whether we want to or not. When we are watching Derek Chauvin's knee on George Floyd's neck for eight minutes and forty-six seconds or witnessing Michael Brown's bullet-ridden body lying on the ground for four and a half hours, we are witnessing more than brutal acts of state violence. We are also being taught a message about the limited value of Black lives, the power of White supremacy, and the state's capacity to determine whether we live or die.

LANGUAGE OF THE UNHEARD

What do you make of the riots that took place in the aftermath of George Floyd's death?

First, we should not use the term *riot* to describe the political resistance that took place in cities across the United States in the aftermath of the George Floyd killing. *Riot* is a word used to frame these actions as random, irrational, and unnecessary acts of violence. Riots would be better applied to the suburban consumers who tear down department stores on Black Friday or the White undergraduates who destroy property after a football game. Of course, we rarely use that language in those instances.

The term *rebellion* is more appropriate because it spotlights organized resistance by the oppressed against the systems that dominate them. The stores that were burned, the police cars that were destroyed, and the statues of White supremacists that were taken down were all part of a strategic effort to challenge a state that continues to kill us with indifference and impunity. These were political acts.

When I say "strategic," I do not mean to overstate or romanticize the way that rebellions occur. Every act in a rebellion isn't the result of strategy sessions and collective consensus. There is a great deal of spontaneity and emotion involved, as well. But these acts are rarely as random, unsophisticated, or self-defeating as they are framed by critics and corporate media.

Although I prefer the term *rebellion* over *riot*, I do so as a way of framing our resistance through a more overtly political lens. This does not mean that the word *riot* is, in itself, morally or politically problematic. In its literal meaning, a riot is a violent public disorder. There is nothing wrong with creating public disorder as a means of resisting state violence, particularly since so much of it happens in the public sphere.

And violence cannot simply be dismissed as a morally unacceptable and strategically ineffective tactic. I believe that we must prioritize and utilize nonviolent strategies. But people have a right to defend themselves against violence, whether from individuals, groups, or the state.

How do you respond to critics who say that the protestors undermined their own success by using non-peaceful methods?

The idea that protestors compromise their moral authority or strategic advantage through violent tactics is equal parts disingenuous, ahistorical, and inaccurate. It's disingenuous to suggest that peaceful tactics are available, yet people simply choose violence. It's inaccurate to suggest that the use of violence is not an effective tool in the fight for freedom. And it's ahistorical to ignore the role that violence, or the threat of violence, has always played in resisting structures of power.

Rebellions are the result of political, moral, and emotional exhaustion. We do not rebel in response to a single act of injustice. If Black people were that reactive, we would be in a constant state of rebellion. We rebel because we have a legitimate distrust—and constant reminders—of the system's capacity to produce justice. We take to the streets because other strategies are dismissed, resisted, or altogether ignored. We craft spectacles of violence as a way of gaining the attention of the powerful, who are otherwise indifferent to our suffering.

When we took to the streets after George Floyd's death, we were responding to more than just his gruesome killing. We were responding to the killing of Ahmaud Arbery, which reminded us of the vulnerability of Black people simply for being outside. We were responding to Amy Cooper, the White woman in Central Park who called the New York City police and, as revenge for being asked to put a leash on her dog, falsely stated that a Black man, Christian Cooper, was threatening her life. We were responding to the execution of Breonna Taylor, who was killed by police as she awakened from sleep. We were responding to the Covid-19 pandemic, which spotlighted our vulnerability and disposability. We were responding to the daily ritual of humiliation, dehumanization, and violence that people experience for being Black, brown, queer, trans, disabled, or undocumented. George Floyd was merely the tipping point.

Martin Luther King once said that "a riot is the language of the unheard." King was explaining that violence was the outcome of the nation's failure to listen to Black protest. But he was also saying that riots were the result of the state's failure to address the structural conditions that consigned Black people to poverty. Although King embraced nonviolence, both as a strategy and personal moral philosophy, he understood that a violent response to injustice was natural and inevitable. We all want peace, but the precondition of peace is, and always will be, justice.

King's philosophy of nonviolence is often invoked as a way of criticizing protestors who use different methods. What lessons can we learn from King?

So many people attempt to water down Martin Luther King's message and work. As a result, we have a public memory of King as an eloquent but docile Negro preacher obsessed with the formation of a colorblind country. In reality, King was not only a gifted preacher but one of the great political strategists of the twentieth century. King did not merely dream about integrated tables, he was committed to reimagining the world in ways that would yield justice for the vulnerable and freedom for the oppressed. King was a pacifist not just against Bull Connor but also against US imperial violence around the globe.

Martin Luther King was not looking to reform the country but to fundamentally change it. King was a radical in the most literal sense: he wanted root-level changes to the whole of society. This required dismantling what King called the "triple evils" of racism, poverty, and militarism.

King wasn't naïve or romantic about the work that needed to be done to realize his dream. He recognized, as Frederick Douglass did long before him, that "power concedes nothing without a demand." He also understood that this demand would not come through the spontaneous moral conversion of the powerful. Rather, it would come from the resistance of the oppressed. King was rooted in, and advanced, the very same Black radical tradition that informs and inspires the radical movements of today.

Still, despite this clear connection, many of our critics and open enemies manipulate King's legacy. In particular, they contrast King's nonviolent approach with the rebellions of 2020. They cite King's political victories as evidence that nonviolent methods work, thereby shaming and discrediting the work of current activists. This approach reflects a simplistic and inaccurate reading of history. Although King practiced nonviolence, his strategy still required the use of violence. When King organizes a nonviolent protest on the Pettus Bridge, he knows that the state is going to do physical harm to the protestors. By not fighting back, and allowing the public to witness the gross spectacle of state violence against unarmed Black people, King and others hoped to marshal the moral authority and sympathy necessary to make political change.

But even as we applaud King for his discipline and moral maturity, as well as his political acumen, it is wholly unreasonable to demand unconditional nonviolence from all oppressed people. The moral authority of the oppressed cannot be conditioned on their commitment to using their own bodies as a ransom for liberation. To do so is to normalize the violence of the oppressor.

To avoid a dishonest reading of history, we must also consider the role of what critical race theorists call "interest convergence." Institutions of power do not simply yield to the demands of the oppressed. Rather, they only do so when they converge with their own interests. With regard to violence, it was easier for the government to acquiesce to King's demands than to negotiate the growing rebellions taking place in the streets, as well as the growing engagement with more radical Black organizations. In many ways, King's effectiveness as a nonviolent leader hinged on the presence and possibility of actual violence.

We cannot ignore the necessary role that violence has played throughout history. Nation-states, by definition, are violent. Empires have always maintained their power through violence. The powerful never yield their power without force, or at least the threat of force. As Malcolm X reminded us in "Message to the Grassroots," there are no nonviolent revolutions. The fundamental question is: Who is worthy of dispensing and receiving violence?

What is different now compared to the first iteration of Black Lives Matter? How is it different from previous movements?

Black Lives Matter is a movement that started in 2013 as a social media hashtag in response to the killing of Trayvon Martin. In 2014, Ferguson, Missouri, became ground zero for a rebellion after the August 9 killing of Michael Brown. By then, the hashtag had evolved into a full-fledged organization, international slogan, and analytical framework for the various forms of violence experienced by Black people.

In 2020, Black Lives Matter signifies many things. People often conflate BLM with the broader Movement for Black Lives, which is a nationwide coalition of groups committed to improving the lives of Black people. BLM has become a political litmus test, uttered by individuals and institutions to assert their belief in the legitimacy and value of Black lives. BLM is now a central feature of American social, cultural, and political life.

It would be a mistake to frame BLM in 2013 and BLM in 2020 as two different movements, or even two iterations of the same movement. Such an approach reduces organizing to the planning of mass protests in the aftermath of high-profile acts of injustice. It limits activism to the spectacles of public unrest captured by corporate media. It presumes that when the cameras, police, and public attention go away, the work of organized resistance stops. In reality, there has been a continual movement of organizing, planning, teaching, and struggling for liberation.

We also must not see the current movement as entirely disconnected from previous movements either. We do ourselves a disservice, both intellectually and strategically, when we lose track of the full arc of our freedom struggle. Since the moment we arrived in the Americas, Black people have been part of an ongoing struggle for liberation. There has never been an interruption in our fight to be free. There has never been a single moment we haven't resisted power. To that extent, we are all part of a singular—though certainly complicated, diverse, and ever-changing—freedom movement.

You say that the freedom movement has been "ever-changing." Can you speak to some of these changes?

For starters, the rebellions of 2020 reveal how drastically our demands have shifted. When I was a teen activist in the 1990s, many of us were calling for abusive cops to be fired or criminally charged. Today, people are calling to defund or abolish police altogether. Unlike prior decades, the folk in the streets do not view political representation as the exclusive, or even primary, mechanism for freedom. They are not fighting to get more Black police chiefs, mayors, and governors. They are looking to fundamentally change the systems that produce them. They are not looking for reform. They want radical transformation.

This generation of freedom fighters also has a far more sophisticated political analysis. They understand that it is not enough to interrupt police violence if we are not willing to engage in a serious critique of capitalism. They are far more willing to embrace an intersectional analysis that takes seriously issues of gender, race, ability, sexual identity, and other critical factors. This does not mean that the current movement isn't shot through with patriarchy, homophobia, transphobia, and ableism. It is. Still, we have developed a far more sophisticated analysis, vocabulary, and political vision than we've ever had before.

I'm also amazed at how the technology has become so much more advanced. The current technological landscape allows us to reimagine what political community and participation look like. Social media has allowed us to exchange information, establish campaigns, and engage in symbolic and concrete forms of resistance that were unavailable even a decade ago. Think about how Cash App and GoFundMe allow for wider forms of grassroots fundraising. Consider how social media allows us to expand our physical and imagined community far more widely. These are just a couple of examples.

The current struggle is increasingly international in scope. Activists are looking around the globe for networks of solidarity and collective resistance. More fundamentally, they are developing more sophisticated understandings of power. They are better able to theorize how structures of domination are not limited by borders or nation-states but are global in both scope and impact.

Of course, most of these shifts are not entirely new. There have always been individuals and groups with sophisticated theory, intersectional analysis, and internationalist vision. I'm speaking about the ways that these energies are increasingly moving from the margin to the center of our movement. For example, defunding the police was a marginal political position held by radical antiprison activists. Today, it has been embraced by influential members of Congress like Ilhan Omar and Alexandria Ocasio-Cortez. Things are moving quickly. We have reason to be hopeful.

Black Lives Matter was born under a Black president, Barack Obama. In hindsight, how do you rate his tenure? Do you think he helped construct the myth that the United States had become truly colorblind?

It is easy to romanticize or misremember the Obama presidency. Between the proto-fascist George W. Bush presidency and the outright fascist Trump presidency, Obama's tenure can look extraordinary by comparison. And the distinction between Obama and his Republican counterparts isn't minor or academic. Still, we cannot afford to forget that Obama was the manager of US empire. Under Obama, the United States engaged in massive drone strikes in Yemen, Somalia, and Pakistan. We funded massive imperial projects around the world. We saw the deportation of more than 2.5 million people. From lead in the water of cities like Flint, Baltimore, and Cleveland to the daily use of excessive force by police, we saw very little substantive response to the various forms of violence suffered by the most vulnerable.

It is worth noting that Obama made several progressive, and perhaps even quasi-abolitionist, moves at the end of his presidency. By ending cash bail and attempting to phase out the privatization of prisons, Obama helped to advance the public and policy discourse on mass incarceration. Still, these were relatively small (and late) gestures, relative to Obama's political power and capacity.

You are right to point out that the Black Lives Matter movement emerged during the Obama presidency. As with George Floyd, the national protests around Trayvon Martin, Michael Brown, and Sandra Bland were not a response to singular incidents but to a pattern of state violence and repression that persisted under Obama's tenure. Some of the most brutal moments of state violence—Eric Garner, Philando Castile, Tamir Rice—happened during the Obama administration. Some of our most desperate and organized cries for the state to stop legally executing us—like the fight to save Troy Davis from the death penalty—happened with Obama as president. Indeed, it was the extreme suffering experienced during the Obama administration that prompted us to the lay the groundwork for the most powerful and sustained movement against state violence in US history.

These conditions are not the fault of Obama per se. After all, he was merely the supervisor of the same project that has exploited and killed us since its creation. Obama's shortcomings and failures were like those of his predecessors and those who follow him. If anything, Obama's presidency is a reminder that we cannot invest our freedom dreams in individual leaders, only in the collective power of the people to imagine and craft new worlds.

We are seeing some incredible events. Statues of former slave traders falling all over the world. Athletes taking a knee with protesters. Soccer teams in the United Kingdom wearing Black Lives Matter T-shirts. Politicians tweeting their support for Black Lives Matter. The danger of cooptation in this moment seems very real.

If I have a concern about the current movement, it is about the potential for cooptation, absolutely. Black Lives Matter can quickly become an empty slogan, and demands for police abolition can turn into watered-down demands for police reform if we are not careful. The managerial class can emerge as leaders of this movement and can be coopted by power brokers in such a way that they misdirect or mislead this movement into liberal irrelevance.

This moment of rebellion is bringing many new people into movement spaces. Many people who were never engaged in radical discourse are witnessing the current moment of militancy and want to be a part of it. The question is: are they joining a movement or do they want the movement to come to them? Do they want the movement on their terms or on the terms of those who are risking their lives while demanding radical outcomes and radical futures?

As soon as people hit the streets in 2020, we saw efforts to coopt the rebellion. News outlets showed images of uniformed police kneeling with protestors. On social media, we saw numerous photos and videos of officers laughing, dancing, and playing basketball with members of the community. These types of representations undermine the radical message of police abolition. They advance the idea that the fundamental problem is not policing itself, but simply the types of police officers who take the job or certain police officers.

This type of cooptation is not just the consequence of liberals joining our movement. There is also a very organized campaign by police to represent themselves as a functional, healthy, and necessary presence in our community. This type of "copaganda" helps to shift the public discourse away from radical ideas and toward reformist ones.

In some cities, the language of the protests has radically shifted. Calls to abolish the police are often being replaced by calls to simply arrest particular officers. Demands to defund police departments are being replaced by requests for community policing, body cameras, and other reformist measures that reinforce the legitimacy and permanence of the police.

We should not be afraid of new people joining the movement. The only way we can strengthen and expand our resistance is by more people becoming politicized and radicalized. But it is important that we engage in the type of political education that allows people to develop an understanding of what's at stake when we make particular choices. Otherwise, I would rather have a smaller number of committed folk who are going to make the demands that get us free than to have a coopted and compromised mass movement that keeps us marching in place.

If we want to turn this movement into a success, what role will Black elected officials play?

To answer your question, look at the city of Baltimore, where Freddie Gray was killed by police in 2015. Nearly half of the officers in the department were Black. There was also a Black mayor, Black city council, and a Black state's attorney, all of whom worked just a few miles away from a Black president. Despite all of this Black elected power, there was still so much Black misery. As Keeanga-Yahmahtta Taylor writes in her brilliant *New York Times* essay "The End of Black Politics," nothing could illustrate more clearly how insufficient Black political power has been to resist the worst dimensions of this White supremacist, capitalist empire.

Think about the emergence of the Congressional Black Caucus around the time George McGovern received the Democratic Party nomination for the presidency, as well as the National Black Political Convention in Gary, Indiana, in 1972. At that time, we viewed political participation and political involvement as a mechanism for expanding Black leadership and ensuring Black liberation. The problem, of course, was that the US political system does not allow for radical or transformative Black leadership. Those Black people who do manage to become elected are often compelled to sell out, often at a cheap price.

The thing about Black elected officials, particularly at the legislative level, is that they are constantly getting elected to get reelected. As a Black politician, you spend so much time spinning your wheels, working with limited resources, and trying to stay in office that you are unable to take radical turns. At the same time, you are forced to make concessions, often with the very people and institutions you were initially trying to challenge.

Black politicians are often not the people best positioned to lead us to liberation. That does not mean, however, that Black politicians cannot play a role. It means that, like all other politicians, they must be directed, they must be challenged, they must be pushed into a set of politics. But we shouldn't assume that our interests will naturally be upheld or advanced through electing Black politicians. Instead, we must demand a political agenda and hold them as accountable as anyone else.

We are talking about the Movement for Black Lives. But another movement, under the leadership of Donald Trump, has gained traction: the movement for White supremacy and fascism. Are you worried that we could be on the verge of a civil war in the United States?

Yes. Donald Trump has certainly fomented White supremacy in this country. Through his rhetoric and policies, he has helped to fertilize the seeds of White resentment, xenophobia, antisemitism, and anti-Blackness. But to focus on this alone is to ignore the ways that White supremacy predates

Trump's tenure. In many ways, Trump did not expand White supremacy. He simply outed it. He has created public space for a block of people who already were privately and secretly supporting White supremacist ideals, if not full-out White supremacist ideology. In some ways what Trump has created is a gift. He has taken all these people who were secretly voting for White supremacy and took them out of hiding. He even put big red hats on them!

When Donald Trump was elected there were many people who were genuinely surprised because they thought we had turned a racial corner. They thought that, in the aftermath of an Obama administration, the country had shown the ability to elect a Black person as its imperial manager, we were no longer bound by the same racial logics, and we were no longer prisoner to White supremacy.

And then Donald Trump comes into office with very clear and unabashed White supremacist narratives, very clear use of anti-Black, anti-woman, antisemitic, and xenophobic images and narratives in his campaign literature. And he gets elected. Fifty-three percent of White women voters voted for Donald Trump, despite the fact that he was caught on video describing gross forms of sexual violence. So at that moment, you saw that White people were willing to close ranks around their Whiteness.

And from that election day forward, Donald Trump has only fanned those flames. In August 2017, the nation witnesses a White nationalist march in Charlottesville, Virginia, that Trump fails to substantively denounce—and even praises. So you have a large block of people who are publicly committed to White supremacy and a White House that is willing to fortify that movement. Against this backdrop, it is no surprise that people in cities around the country are holding weapons to defend Confederate flags or the statues of slave owners and colonizers.

These people are willing to shed blood to defend Whiteness. For this reason, there is absolutely potential not only for civil unrest but full-out civil war. I pray that it does not happen, but this is a distinct and terrifying possibility.

How should White people stand in solidarity with Black people? How can they be true antiracists?

Ibram X. Kendi gives us an important framing for this. He says that everyone is either racist or antiracist. That means it is not enough to not be racist, which is a passive identity. You have to be active against racism.

For White people, solidarity means actively fighting to destroy White supremacy. Solidarity means moving beyond symbolic gestures. Wearing T-shirts and placing signs in our front yards is not enough. Where do we spend our money? Are we donating to the bail funds of those Black people on the ground resisting and getting arrested? Are we donating to organizations that are actively trying to dismantle these oppressive systems? Are we willing to compromise our own power and privilege? If a White person wants to stand in solidarity, what are they willing to give up?

A core piece of solidarity is going to communities of color and asking what they need. Very often, White allies offer what they think people want, what they themselves would want, or what they think is best. Without input from the communities you are trying to support, this is paternalistic. Instead of saying "Here's what I'm going to do," White allies should ask, "What do you need?" "How can I support you?" This shift in approach is critical.

Solidarity means being willing to organize in your own community. Do not try and lead our movements. Go lead your own against White supremacy. It is not enough to come to my Black Lives Matter march. I want you to organize one in your community, in your neighborhood. It is not enough to tell me that you hate racism. I need you to be courageous in White spaces where no one is watching.

I have White activists come to me and talk about how racist their family members are, and how they hate going home for Thanksgiving because their uncle makes racist jokes. But if they say nothing to the racist uncle to challenge them, their silence becomes complicity. For White allies, the question isn't simply *if* they are willing to be courageous. They must also consider *where* they are willing to be courageous.

True ally-ship requires people to be self-critical and introspective. Do not presume that because you believe that White supremacy is bad, and that you are not holding on to White supremacist logic and practices in your own lived experience, your work is done. You also have to be willing to engage in deep self-examination at all times. You need to be committed to keeping track all of your various biases and phobias. You must make sure that you are unlearning Whiteness every day. You also have to be willing to accept critique.

For many allies, this is the most challenging part of solidarity work. It is often the White ally who, when challenged or critiqued, gets defensive and tries to justify or explain away their actions. Sometimes they become dismissive, or use their intentions as a shield from legitimate criticism: "But I'm on your side!" "Why are you picking on me?" "Why not worry about the real racist over there?" In doing so, they reinforce a certain kind of paternalism that makes it difficult to forge real bonds of solidarity.

Angela Davis, who has seen her share of struggles and movements, said recently that she had never seen a movement like the one in response to George Floyd's murder. Keeanga-Yamahtta Taylor calls this "the broadest protest movement in US history." Are we at a turning point, in your opinion?

In every moment of rebellion, there are possibilities for cooptation and counterinsurgency. Victory is never certain. But what we are seeing right now is the kind of mass action, political clarity, and radical imagination that always animates the most successful movements. The possibilities are rich. I'm deeply hopeful.

JUSTICE FOR "ALL"

I'm hearing many activists not only say "Black Lives Matter" but that "All Black Lives Matter?" I've also heard you say this many times. Why is this distinction important?

"All Black Lives Matter" is a critical phrase. The word "all" serves as a reminder that Black people must be defended and protected, regardless of the identities they carry, the bodies they inhabit, the decisions they make, or the conditions in which they find themselves. "All Black Lives Matter" is a declaration that no one is disposable.

When we affirm the value of all Black lives, we are including those who do not fit into mainstream frameworks of respectability. As soon as a Black person is the victim of state violence, the government and its defenders attempt to justify its violence by attacking the person's character. When Trayvon Martin was killed, media outlets and George Zimmerman's attorneys pored through his school records to frame him as a bad person. When Mike Brown was killed, they tried to focus on the cigarillo that he stole from a store, even though Darren Wilson was unaware of this fact when he stopped him for jaywalking. When Black women and queer Black men are killed while engaged in sex work, many point to their underground labor as the justification for their death.

This preoccupation with respectability is not just applied to Black people from the outside but also emerges from within the community. Nine months before Rosa Parks made history by refusing to surrender her Montgomery, Alabama, bus seat to a White person, Claudette Colvin did the very same thing. But since Colvin was a pregnant and unmarried teenager, whose skin color and hair texture did not meet the standards of White America or the Black bourgeoisie, her historic action was largely ignored by the civil rights establishment. They feared that Colvin's personal life would make her a "bad girl" in the eyes of the public and compromise the moral authority they believed was necessary to demand social change.

Sadly, not much has changed since 1955. We continue to present Black victims as perfect in order to justify our cries of justice. We show images of Trayvon Martin on a horse. We declare that Michael Brown was set to begin college the Monday he was killed. We highlight Christian Cooper's Harvard University pedigree to bolster our outrage at Amy Cooper's racist police report. Of course, some of these choices are strategic. Effective political organizing requires us to appeal to the sensibilities of the public to garner sympathy and build outrage. But these decisions also reflect our own deeply rooted disdain for those living on the margins of society.

By focusing on all Black lives, we affirm that our humanity does not hinge on our social acceptability, respectability, or proximity to power. This means that we fight for Trayvon Martin whether he rides horses or smokes marijuana. We demand accountability for the murder of Michael Brown even though he stole from a store. We should feel the same outrage against Amy Cooper if she had called the police on a gang member rather than an Ivy League birder. We must acknowledge sex work as a legitimate form of labor that does not deprive a person of dignity, safety, and protection.

A focus on All Black Lives means that we must also fight for those who do harm to us. In the aftermath of George Floyd's killing, conservatives like Candace Owens pointed to Floyd's criminal history as proof that our protests in his defense were misguided. We can have moral critiques of the neighborhood drug dealer, the person who robs houses, or someone incarcerated for a violent crime. These critiques cannot, however, lead us to ignore injustices against those who do harm within our communities. Such a position yields the lives of those we deem "bad people" to the violence of the state. It also denies the possibility of healing, redemption, and transformation. Instead, we must create mechanisms for holding individuals accountable for their actions while asserting their fundamental right to love, investment, and protection.

All Black Lives Matter is a call to understand Black life through the lens of intersectionality. We must understand that race, gender, and sexual identity are all factors that shape how we negotiate the world, as well as how the world responds to us. All Black Lives Matter reminds us that no particular configuration of these categories should lead to the refusal or failure to protect us.

All. Black Lives Matter is an analytic framework that forces us to look at the particular levels of precarity that we experience as a consequence of our particular intersecting identities. We have to look at the very particular ways that harm is done to Black trans women. We have to look at the very particular ways that Black women and girls are affected by state violence.

In a way, the "all" has always been there. From the moment that Alicia Garza, Patrisse Cullors, and Opal Tometi created Black Lives Matter, they were articulating a vision of freedom that kept track of every single person within the Black community. There was never a moment when they weren't thinking about women, queer folk, trans sibs, people with disabilities, undocumented family, and other people who live on the margins of various communities. This speaks to the moral clarity of their vision as well as the significance of the intellectual and political traditions that anchor them.

Black Lives Matter is rooted in not only the Black radical tradition but also the Black feminist tradition. As Barbara Ransby reminds us in her brilliant book *Making All Black Lives Matter*, we often acknowledge the first, but too often ignore the second.

Why has Black feminism been so important?

Black feminism is the political, intellectual, and moral anchor of our freedom struggle. Black women, and specifically Black feminists, have consistently theorized, organized, and struggled for the most ambitious and inclusive freedom dreams possible. Radical Black feminists have not only struggled to end patriarchy but to produce a world devoid of all forms of oppression. Look at the Combahee River Collective statement of 1974, which Keeanga-Yamahtta Taylor brilliantly analyzes in her book *How We Get Free*. In the document, this group of radical Black feminists laid out a politics that demanded an end to gender-based oppression but also called for the dismantling of capitalism, an end to imperialism, and solidarity with the Third World.

The sad irony, of course, is that Black women have engaged in these inclusive forms of world-making at the same time that they have been placed at the bottom of the social ladder. As we have struggled for freedom, we have largely ignored issues of misogyny, patriarchy, homophobia, and transphobia. This has played out in terms of our political vision, leadership models, tactics, and interpersonal interactions. At the same time that Black women have fought to free all of us, we have continued to fight for a world that prioritizes the lives of cisgendered heterosexual Black men.

Has that historical tendency continued to play out in the present movement?

Absolutely. Of course, we have made tremendous improvements. The fact that so many of our most powerful movements are led by women, queer and trans folk, and other people who are not cis-hetero Black men is a testament to our progress. Our political demands are far more inclusive than ever before. The current generation of activists has a much more progressive gender and sexual identity politics.

It would be dishonest to ignore the developments we have made. Still, there remains a huge gap between our most radical freedom dreams and our actual political demands. There is too sharp a contradiction between our political ideologies and our lived practice. Even as we fight for an inclusive freedom movement, we continue to enact transphobia, heteropatriarchy, ableism, and other violent ideologies that undermine our political and moral consistency.

Can you give some example of where this has happened?

Let's start with the case of Breonna Taylor, a Black woman killed by Louisville police on March 13, 2020, while they were executing a "no-knock" warrant. When the police entered her home early in the morning, Taylor's boyfriend, Kenneth Walker, believed that they were intruders and fired a single shot from his gun. The police responded by firing more than twenty-five rounds. Despite being unarmed and posing no apparent threat to police, Taylor was shot eight times by Officer Brett Hankison, who recklessly fired ten shots into the covered patio door. Although the charges were later dismissed, Walker was initially charged with attempted murder of a police officer.

The Breonna Taylor case had all the elements needed to spark mainstream outrage and national protest. She was unarmed in her own home. She was not involved in illegal activity. She was a first responder, working as an emergency medical technician. While these factors should not matter—Taylor shouldn't have been killed if she were unemployed or sold drugs—they are often used as excuses not to fight for justice.

But in this case, Taylor met all of the bourgeois liberal standards of the "worthy victim." So why was there so little response after her death? Why did it take the death of George Floyd to spark national outrage and protest? Some will argue that our silence around Taylor was due to the absence of video footage. Of course, the lack of audiovisual evidence certainly makes it harder to garner public sympathy, as the spectacle of violence is so often a critical element. But we can't accept that as an excuse. After all, we fought for Trayvon Martin and Michael Brown without video evidence. And even though we had audio of Sandra Bland, her death didn't generate a comparable movement. This reality speaks to the way that Black women, girls, and femmes are marginalized within our current movement.

Throughout US history, our movements for justice have been animated by the beating or killling of cisgender heterosexual Black men. Emmett Till in 1955, Rodney King in 1992, Trayvon Martin in 2012, Mike Brown in 2014, George Floyd in 2020. Each case became the rallying cry for justice.

Whenever Black death or brutalization has called us to action, the body has been gendered male and, given the heteronormative framework of our society, we have presumed them to be heterosexual.

Conversely, there has never been a moment where the deaths of Black women, girls, or femmes has inspired a comparable response. There was little public discussion of Kathryn Johnston, a ninety-two-year-old Black woman killed by Atlanta police during an illegal drug raid and then posthumously framed by officers for drug possession with the intent to sell. The death of Renisha McBride, a Black woman shot in the face in 2013 after knocking on the door of a Detroit house when she was looking for help after a car accident, barely made a blip on the media and activist radar. At no moment in history have we been able to find inspiration for collective resistance in the harmed body of a Black woman, girl, or femme.

If we are to truly embrace the belief that All Black Lives Matter, this must be modeled in our activism. The deaths of cis-hetero Black men at the hands of police is something we cannot ignore. But it can't be the only story.

What about those who say that Black men are the primary victims of state violence?

First, that is simply untrue. Black women experience state violence in multiple ways. They are the victims of abusive language, excessive physical abuse, and unlawful arrests far more than their White counterparts, though even these measures themselves are part of the problem.

Too often, we only measure the crisis of state violence through the lens of Black male experience. To really ensure that All Black Lives Matter, we must consider the ways that women, girls, and femmes experience violence at the hands of the state. For example, studies show that Black men are often perceived by police, as well as the broader society, to be naturally stronger, less rational, and more prone to violence. These perceptions are directly linked to the use of force against them by police. We often fail to consider, however, how these White supremacist narratives impact Black women. Since slavery, Black women have been portrayed or perceived as "masculine" or "man-like." When Black women, girls, and femmes display behavior that is deemed "unlady-like" or otherwise does not comport with gendered standards of behavior, they are much more likely to be arrested. They have never been granted the fraught protections of patriarchy from the police, who often avoid violent interactions with White women because of their perceived gentleness and fragility. Simply put, Black women often get read like Black men and treated like Black men by the police.

But we must also look at the specific narratives about Black women that inform their experiences with state violence, not merely the ones that operate in relation to Black men. Since slavery, Black women have been framed as dishonest, hypersexual, and immoral. These factors increase the chances that Black women will be viewed with suspicion and distrust by police. A Black woman standing on the corner rarely receives the benefit of the doubt in the eyes of the state or in the public imagination. Instead, she is viewed as a sex worker or drug user whose moral failures justify whatever violence she experiences.

We must also look at the pervasive sexual violence experienced by Black women, girls, and femmes, who are much more likely to be sexually assaulted during their interactions with police. They are also more likely to experience sexual violence in jails, prisons, and juvenile detention centers than their male counterparts.

I notice that you have repeatedly said "women, girls, and femmes." Can you talk about why you stress these identities?

If we are to truly embrace the belief that All Black Lives Matter, then we have to keep track of the most marginalized members of our community. This means that, even as we highlight the experiences of women, we shouldn't only focus on cisgendered women. We need to include all woman-identified and femme-presenting people, including nonbinary folk, within our framework. This is not just a political gesture, but a recognition that patriarchal state violence is an experience shared by everyone who presents or is read as "female."

Even as we talk about the experiences of women, we must pay particular attention to the lives of trans women. Trans women, particularly Black trans women, are often viewed through the lens of criminality. A Black trans woman walking down the street is often assumed to be a sex worker, and subject to unlawful stops and arrests. They are also much more likely to be sexually harassed or assaulted by the police officers who stop them.

For trans folk, the violence of the state becomes even more severe after incarceration. Look at the case of CeCe McDonald, a Black trans woman in Minnesota, who was charged and convicted of manslaughter after stabbing someone in self-defense during a transphobic attack. McDonald was sentenced to forty-one months of incarceration in a men's prison. This is a common experience of incarcerated trans populations. They are typically misgendered throughout the legal process, identified by their "dead name" rather than their chosen name, and subjected to pronouns that deny the legitimacy of their gender identity.

And the impacts are not merely psychological. Trans men and women are often denied proper medical treatment and placed in solitary confinement for long periods of time. When trans women are placed in men's prisons, they are exponentially more likely to be sexually assaulted. Given these conditions, the presence of trans people in prison generally constitutes cruel and unusual punishment.

Is it about patriarchy, as well? We are a male-dominated world, and patriarchy is a form of oppression, of violence, that is ingrained even into many social justice activists.

Patriarchy is a key explanatory factor here. Patriarchy is the reason that we fail to understand and take seriously the experiences of Black women and girls. The logics of patriarchy make the male experience not only the dominant experience but often the singular one. We have always measured Black pain by its impact on Black men. We are unable to think outside that oppressive framework and, as a result, we lose sight of the wide range of ways that state violence presents itself. For example, we pay careful attention to the mass incarceration of Black men, and all the accompanying criminal justice processes, as examples of state violence.

To move beyond a patriarchal analysis, we must do more than just consider the experiences of women within the modern prison regime. We must also locate other spaces of structural violence that do not place men at the center. As Matthew Desmond teaches in his book *Evicted,* Black women experience housing evictions at a disproportionately high rate. Like mass incarceration, evictions are the product of institutional racism, unregulated capitalism, and government disinvestment. Evictions destabilize families and undermine access to living wages, food security, healthy relationships, and social mobility. In order to understand how racial capitalism impacts Black life, we must look at Black women's evictions just as much as we examine Black men's convictions.

Housing is just one example. Black women are two to three times more likely to die from pregnancy-related causes than White women. Eighty percent of Black women will suffer from fibroids by the age of fifty. As scholar Mark Anthony Neal once pointed out, most Black men are unaware of this. Can you imagine any medical issue experienced by 80 percent of Black men that Black women wouldn't know about? This speaks to the need for us to decenter the perspectives of cis-hetero men and hold space for the narratives, experiences, and identities of those consigned to the margins.

Without question, Black cis-hetero men are victims of a racist and violent system. But this fact does not nullify the reality that we are also tremendous perpetrators of harm within our community. For example, many interactions between police and Black men stem from domestic violence complaints. While we may have legitimate critiques of the particular ways that police intervene, we cannot ignore the equally critical crisis of Black male violence against women.

Similarly, we cannot critique state violence against Black trans women without acknowledging that they are far more likely to be killed by a Black man than by the police. To truly affirm that All Black Lives Matter, we must be willing to acknowledge our power and privilege, recognize our complicity with systems of oppression, and work to undo and avoid repeating the harm we have caused.

Since we're talking about the word all, *can you also talk about the phrase "All Lives Matter" used by many Whites and critics of BLM? Why is this phrase problematic?*

First, we must unpack the meaning of the term *all*. In the abstract, *all* is a word that suggests universality and inclusivity. It's a word that speaks to democratic possibilities. But language is never neutral. Language is always political. And the word *all* is no exception. While some are using it as a way of spotlighting the humanity and fundamental value of all people, others are using the phrase "All Lives Matter" as a way of undermining those very same goals.

So the issue isn't the term *all*, but rather the political context in which it is being used. The declaration "All Lives Matter" is not inherently problematic. In fact, to the contrary, it *could* be a powerful affirmation of all human beings. But we cannot ignore when and how the "All Lives Matter" ideology has been invoked. Given the history of violence against Black people in the United States, there is something deeply disingenuous about White people suddenly declaring that all lives matter.

America has had four hundred years to say "All Lives Matter." When Black people were stolen and enslaved, White people could have abolished the project of slavery by saying, "Wait, no, all lives matter." Whites could have interrupted the lynch mobs and stopped the extrajudicial killing of innocent Black people by saying, "Do not hang these people from trees because all lives matter." When Black people were subjected to legalized apartheid from 1896 until 1954, from *Plessy v. Ferguson* to *Brown v. Board of Education*, US citizens could have intervened and said, "No, we need an equal legal system because all lives matter." There have been numerous instances in US history when White people had the ability, with complete moral authority, to say all lives matter—but they never did.

Today is no different. As Arab and Muslim and Latinx refugees are denied safe haven, as immigrant children are placed in cages or separated from their families, as the elderly and the poor are being subjected to unnecessary exposure to Covid-19, the nation could resist these cruel policies by declaring "All Lives Matter." But this country has yet to do this. It is only at the moment when Black people assert the specific legitimacy of their lives in response to the systematic devaluing of their lives that we want to become universal in response to a very particular problem.

"All Lives Matter" is not an appeal to universality. It is a response to the Movement for Black Lives. The point of this slogan is to dishonestly frame Black Lives Matter as a movement that is not committed to protecting and asserting the value of all human life. "All Lives Matter" also ignores the ways that Black life has been especially and unnecessarily vulnerable throughout US history. If all lives mattered in this country, we would not be risking our lives fighting for freedom, dignity, and justice.

WHOSE VIOLENCE?

In the United States, the police kill almost three people every day, which is more than one thousand people every year. What do these numbers tell you?

The number of people killed by police in the United States is quite stunning. Based on the latest data, police kill 33.5 per 10 million people here. In 2019, 1,099 civilians were killed by police officers. When we break the numbers down by race, they become even more disturbing. According to a study published in the *American Journal of Public Health*, Black men are three times more likely, and Latino men are 40 percent more likely, to be killed by police than White men.

It is also important to place these numbers in global context. In comparison to the 33.5 per 10 million people killed in the United States, other countries' rates are quite low: Canada, 9.8; Australia, 8.5; The Netherlands, 2.3; New Zealand, 2.0; Germany, 1.3; England and Wales, 0.5; Japan, 0.2; Iceland, 0; Norway, 0. These numbers affirm the fact US police pose an existential threat to the most vulnerable people. They also show that this is not inevitable.

Some will say that police violence is simply the unavoidable consequence of being a modern nation-state. But how, then, can we explain the fact that US police kill people at rates exponentially higher than Germany, Canada, or the United Kingdom? To answer this, we must address the specific historical, political, and cultural factors that cause the United States to have such extraordinarily high numbers of police violence.

The cruel irony is that the more heavily you are policed, the more vulnerable you are to violence. For this reason, it is no surprise that US police kill more people than other countries. To understand police violence, we must first understand the history of US policing. Modern policing is directly connected to the violent formation of the nation-state. Just as we cannot understand the United States outside the context of slavery, we can't make sense of modern policing without locating its roots within this "peculiar institution." As Angela Davis teaches us in *Are Prisons Obsolete?*, the practice of modern policing is rooted in early slave patrols.

Enslaved Africans were legally the property of slave owners. Part of why you did not see mass killings of Africans during the time of legal slavery was because we were property. Slave masters would not kill an enslaved person any more readily than they would destroy their own pick, shovel, or ax. Of course, they would routinely use violence as a means of controlling, disciplining, and terrorizing enslaved

Africans, and especially to prevent revolts, but the fundamental goal was to maintain their property and sustain their business. This is where slave patrols became indispensable.

Slave patrols were groups of White citizen volunteers who would track down and return enslaved Africans who ran away. They would enforce slave codes and quell slave rebellions. Slave patrols were the first instantiation of the modern police force, whose primary purpose has never been to protect and serve the broader public but to protect the interests and property of the powerful. While they protected the specific interests of individual slave owners, they helped to sustain the broader American project.

Modern policing in the United States is a continuation of the same project of protecting the powerful. As Sidney L. Harring notes in his classic book *Policing a Class Society,* the primary function of the police has never been to protect the general public from crime and violence or to advance any conception of justice. Since the end of the Civil War, police have been a key mechanism used by the ruling class to accumulate capital by managing the behavior, the resistance, and even the leisure of the working class. Their primary function has been to manage working-class dissent and enforce laws that sustain the economic status quo.

An excellent example of this came during the May 2020 protests in Minnesota against the killing of George Floyd. President Trump tweeted a clear warning to protestors: "When the looting starts, the shooting starts." Of course, we must also be clear that Trump's willingness to deploy violence against protestors was also due to the fact that so many of them were Black. In fact, the particular phrase he used was taken (without attribution) from former Miami police chief Walter Headley, who made the statement in 1967 in response to civil rights protests. Like Headley, Trump was both threatening Black dissenters and sending a racist dog whistle to his political base.

Still, Trump's words were only a more crude and transparent articulation of what the powerful have always shown us: the state's fundamental priority is to protect the interests of the ruling class at all costs, even if the price is human life. And we have normalized this logic in every aspect of US culture.

What are some areas of US culture where this is normalized?

For starters, we don't historicize policing. In school, we don't teach about the origin or development of the police as an institution, or acknowledge that police haven't existed for most of human history. As a result, we are encouraged to believe that a world without police is both unprecedented and impossible.

From childhood, we are taught to valorize the police. Neighborhood and schoolyard games like "Cops and Robbers" teach us to view the police as the "good guys" regardless of context. As a result, we learn to view issues like crime and policing in very flat, Manichean terms. This makes it extremely difficult to develop a critical posture toward the police or a sympathetic response to someone who breaks a law. Such complexity is needed to challenge a police officer who engages in misconduct or to recognize the moral complexity of someone who sells drugs or steals out of economic desperation or in order to survive.

Media and popular culture have been key in transforming the police into heroes within our collective imagination. While early media representations of the police were unfavorable—think about the Keystone Cops—modern Hollywood has been committed to reinforcing the notion of the cop as hero. Television dramas like *Law & Order* frame the police as hard-working agents of justice, often undermined by shady defense attorneys who allow the "bad guys" to elude the criminal justice process. Movies like *Bad Boys* and *Lethal Weapon* frame the police as sincere, principled, and likable people whose intentions and fundamental humanity are more important than their policing practices. Reality shows like *Cops*, which aired for thirty-one years before being officially canceled in June 2020, represent the police as noble saviors who face unimaginable levels of danger while pursuing justice within largely Black, brown, and poor communities.

These cultural practices do not merely encourage us to valorize the police. They also prepare us to perpetually grant police the benefit of the doubt. They compel us to justify police misconduct as a necessary evil. If we believe the police are fighting uphill against legal technicalities, we are more likely to accept when they plant evidence or give false testimony in order to catch a criminal. If we are constantly shown images of police "getting a little rough" with suspects in order to prove their guilt, then we come to accept police violence as an unavoidable part of their job. If we are fed a steady diet of Black and brown criminality, we begin to view heavy and aggressive policing as justified.

What role do guns play in this conversation?

We live in a country that worships guns. From politics to popular culture, we are taught to view guns as the embodiment of our liberty. We are taught to see the right to bear arms granted by the Second Amendment as the most powerful reflection and protection of democracy. We are taught to believe that an armed police force and an armed citizenry are key to preserving peace, safety, and justice.

But the impact of guns is not just symbolic or abstract. In the United States, more than 400 million guns are in circulation. That means that there are literally more guns than people in this country. Research shows that, regardless of income level, there is a correlation between access to guns and the level of violent crime. Gun ownership increases the likelihood of violence against both civilians and police.

Still, despite these indisputable facts, the political establishment refuses to commit to reducing the number of available guns. Instead, the state has simply decided to enhance the volume and power of its own weaponry. US police have essentially decided to escalate.

Baltimore police, along with hundreds of others from Florida, New Jersey, Pennsylvania, California, Arizona, Connecticut, New York, Massachusetts, North Carolina, Georgia, Washington State, and the DC Capitol Police, have gone for training in Israel. Israel is a state that has used repressive means toward its minority populations and the Palestinian people. It has been in constant violation of international law for half a century. How does this relationship impact the police violence we're seeing?

Since the September 11 attacks, there has been an increase in police exchange programs between police departments in the United States and Israel. These exchanges are incredibly important and worth examining.

First, it would be wrong to suggest that US police were taught how to kill, or otherwise engage in acts of violence, by Israel. The United States has been a violent and repressive nation-state since its inception, long before Israel's establishment in 1948. Blaming Israel for the extrajudicial killings of Black people in the United States not only ignores the deep history of state violence here, but also reinforces, whether intentionally or unintentionally, the longstanding antisemitic canard of the blood libel, in which Jewish people are falsely blamed for the deaths of non-Jewish people. In a moment of rising antisemitism, it is crucial that we make this clear.

At the same time, we shouldn't ignore the significance of police exchange programs between the United States and Israel. We must examine how this specific relationship reflects broader trends in both countries. Israel trains its police with a counterterrorism approach. This is because the Israeli state views all Palestinians—whether they live in Israel, East Jerusalem, the West Bank, Gaza, or throughout the diaspora—as potential terrorists. This counterterrorism mentality allows police to justify tactics like preemptive striking, shooting before they shoot you. It encourages police to view the people they police as outside threats rather than people whom they are supposed to protect and serve.

As we witnessed in the streets of Ferguson in 2014, and even more so during Trump's federal response to the protests of 2020, the US government has increasingly responded to civilian protests with the type of militarism typically reserved for foreign threats. Black and brown communities have been the primary sites of this type of militarism. This approach is accompanied by other proto-fascist moves like demonizing the press and framing all dissent as subversive.

We are also watching the use of military-grade weapons by local police. Many of these weapons are produced and exported to the United States by Israel. So it is not surprising that we see police carrying scaled-down versions of the Uzi submachine gun. Israel also has police training academies in the United States, in Arizona and Georgia, providing tactical weapons training.

We must also examine the way that the United States has increasingly adopted Israel's concept of the security state. Within a security state, the prioritization of security becomes the justification for all other state practices. Democracy, human rights, and privacy are viewed as legitimate and desirable, but only to the extent that they don't compromise state security.

In the two decades since 9/11, we have seen the expansion of the US security state through the same logic that has governed Israel since its creation. As we are subjected to increased government surveillance and intensified attacks on our civil liberties, the government reminds us that "we are surrounded by terror," "there is danger everywhere," and "if you have done nothing wrong, you have nothing to worry about."

Given these trends, police exchanges between the United States and Israel cannot be properly understood as one-sided or purely causal. As each country becomes more authoritarian under the respective administrations of Donald Trump and Benjamin Netanyahu, they are leaning on their close relationship as means of information sharing and strategy building. This relationship has only reinforced a longstanding trend toward antidemocratic government and militaristic policing in the United States.

When we see the police on the streets of US cities today, it is really hard to tell the difference between them and the army.

During the 2014 protests in Ferguson, the police used tanks, grenade launchers, and high-end security equipment that looked like something out of a futuristic Hollywood movie. I asked myself: How could the same town that didn't have dashboard cameras have this much high-tech equipment?

How could a small suburban town, with so few residents and police officers, have the capacity for this scale of response?

And Ferguson is hardly exceptional. Look at Ada, Oklahoma, which has a population of only sixteen thousand. The Ada police department has a total of ten officers, only eight of them full-time. In July 2019, Ada received a mine-resistant armored car. They currently are in possession of thirty-four M-16s. This means that they have four times as many M-16s as full-time police officers.

This militarization of local police departments has occurred through a series of deliberate policy decisions that expanded the volume and type of equipment to which these departments have access. The most influential policy decision was the creation of the 1033 Program in 1997. Since then, the US government has given $8.6 billion in military equipment, from guns to helicopters to tanks, to more than eight thousand police forces around the country. The program was stopped under Barack Obama but, unsurprisingly, was revived under Donald Trump in 2017. That year alone, 500 million pieces of military equipment were given to police departments around the country.

But why do these small towns need this kind of weaponry? In fact, why does any police department need this level of weaponry? In truth, there is absolutely no legitimate reason. By allowing this level of militarization, we enable cities, even small ones, to wage war against their own residents. We also tacitly encourage police departments to overreact to civil unrest and deploy excessive force.

You've spoken about how the spectacle of George Floyd's killing created public outrage. But it also sparked a public conversation about the nature of policing itself.

Without question, the killing of George Floyd, as well as that of Breonna Taylor, helped to shift the public conversation. Rather than merely focusing on their specific deaths, we have been forced to acknowledge the ordinariness of police violence. Black women and men are subjected to excessive police force daily. Even when you account for the nature of our suspected crimes—presuming that physical force may be more necessary for an armed gunman than a petty thief—Black and brown people experience non-lethal excessive police force at a 50 percent higher rate than White people. Our lifetime risk of death by police violence is more than 1.5 times greater than that of white people.

Although the spectacle of death prompts us to take action, that can sometimes be a distraction from the more fundamental problem of everyday police violence. Otherwise, we are encouraged to believe that the cases of Floyd and Taylor are tragic acts of police violence that are an exception to ordinary policing. The story of US police violence is not "Sometimes violent police kill us." The more accurate narrative is "US policing is a violent institution that uses illegal and excessive force against its most vulnerable citizens routinely. Sometimes, in the process of engaging in ritual violence against us, they also kill us."

Numerous people have had their homes raided by heavily

armed police officers, as in the case of Breonna Taylor. Like George Floyd, countless Black people have found themselves on the receiving end of a police officer's knee to their neck or some other comparable form of brutality. The only difference with these two cases is that they killed someone while using "excessive" force, and they were caught on video while killing someone. Within the logic of US policing, the officers did something extraordinary while engaged in practices that are entirely ordinary.

These ordinary forms of police violence do considerable harm to our minds, bodies, and spirits. They normalize repression. They undermine our resistance. And they legitimize the state's right to use violence, including lethal violence.

You say that we legitimize the state's right to use violence. But the focus on police brutality has led many people to call for an end to state violence.

Without question, the protests of 2020 have amplified the call to end state violence. But there is a difference between challenging forms of state violence and raising more fundamental questions about the state's right to use violence, which we almost never do. For example, we may ask the US government to better regulate its violence—to end the death penalty, a particular war, or police brutality—but we rarely call into question its authority to dispense violence.

So when we call for nonviolence, we are not demanding peace. We are demanding passivity from the people. We are calling for a world in which the state is the only entity that uses physical force. This is not particular to the United States or even the West. As sociologist Max Weber argued in his classic 1919 essay "Politics as a Vocation," the monopoly on the legitimate use of violence is one of the defining characteristics of the modern state. This stands in contrast to previous eras, such as feudalism, when not even a king could declare an absolute monopoly over physical force. Even as vassals pledged their allegiance to the king, they also were able to deploy force as a means of managing their individual fiefdoms. It is only the modern state that possesses the exclusive right to violence. States that do not effectively manage this right are often viewed as insufficiently modern or completely illegitimate.

Given its violent history, how could anyone justify the idea of the US state having an exclusive right to violence?

While the United States certainly has a long history of violence that stands in sharp contrast to its self-image and expressed history, it would be misleading to frame this as a unique contradiction. No country, state, or empire in human history could morally justify the right to violence. The modern nation-state—which is invariably and unavoidably the product of violence, dislocation, and erasure—is no exception. There is simply no such thing a nonviolent state, whether in the abstract or in practice.

That said, the monopoly of violence argument is rooted in particular notions of legitimacy. The idea that only government violence is legitimate is based on the presumption that the government will only dispense violence when absolutely necessary, for example, to protect its citizens or defend its territorial integrity. Defenders of this idea argue that the state must possess the capacity to use violence in order to sustain the state itself. To accept such an idea, however, we must believe that the state has the moral authority and political will to appropriately dispense violence. We must trust that the state will recognize and protect the interests of its citizens. Of course, history has shown us otherwise in every nation-state around the world. The United States, despite its desperate attempts to suggest otherwise, is not exceptional.

TOWARD AN ABOLITIONIST VISION

we are each other's
harvest:
we are each other's
business:
we are each other's
magnitude and bond.
　　　　—Gwendolyn Brooks, "Paul Robeson"

As I reflect on the current moment, I see a widening sky of possibility. The public sphere is filled with radical voices, radical ideas, and radical action. We are dreaming together, envisioning a free and safe world where we finally turn *to* each rather than *on* each other.

If we have learned anything from this moment of Covid-19, it is that we cannot survive a crisis through individual action and practice. It means nothing for me to wear my mask if you don't wear yours. It means nothing for me to establish social distance if you walk up in my space. For me to be safe, you have to be safe. This is what Martin Luther King Jr. meant when he said, "We are caught in an inescapable network of mutuality, tied in a single garment of destiny. Whatever affects one directly affects all indirectly." This sensibility must guide us through not only the crisis of Covid-19 but also the crisis of living within a fascist, White supremacist, patriarchal, capitalist empire in decline.

In the midst of loss and death and suffering, our charge is to figure out what freedom really means—and what our next move is to get there. I don't mean a specific tactic or strategy but the larger vision that we are to embrace. Historian Robin D. G. Kelley talks about "freedom dreams," which speaks to the need to conjure the radical imagination in order to do the work of liberation. At this moment, we must ask ourselves, what does freedom *actually* look like? What does justice require? What will the future demand of us to one day declare victory?

The answer to these questions comes through an abolitionist vision. When I speak of an abolitionist vision, I am speaking to the beautifully audacious freedom dreams described by Angela Davis, Ruth Wilson Gilmore, Mariame Kaba, Joy James, and so many other brilliant and courageous Black women. They teach us that, to be truly free, we must struggle to create a world where harm is met with restoration, justice is not confused with punishment, and safety is not measured by the number of human beings we imprison. They teach us that a world of police and prisons and cages is not free or humane or sustainable.

But an abolitionist vision is about more than dismantling the prison. It is also about building a world where we work together to meet one another's needs; a world built on communities of care and networks of nurture; a world in which every living being has access to safety, self-determination, freedom, and dignity.

This moment of rebellion has spotlighted the harm caused by our collective investment in blame and punishment rather than restoration and healing. All of the money spent to reform the police, enhance the punishment state, and build more prisons did not protect George Floyd and Breonna Taylor. It never could. Their tragic deaths reinforced what abolitionists already knew: the problem with policing isn't one of good versus bad apples. Our crisis is not rooted in the actions of particular police but the institution of policing itself, which cannot be disentangled from its origins as a mechanism for surveilling, criminalizing, punishing, and killing Black bodies.

Some are leveraging this moment to call for criminal justice reform. These measures are designed to coerce us into believing the lie that the prison and its entangled institutions are salvageable, that the institution of policing is fixable, and that the system of capitalism is regulatable. But the truth has been laid bare again and again. They are not. What will secure us is embracing an abolitionist imagination that forces us beyond the posture of reform and dares us to imagine a world of new possibilities.

The architectures that uphold prisons have absorbed resources that could have been used to provide for the health care needs of a nation in crisis. Instead, the incarcerated were used to make masks and hand sanitizer that they were not allowed to use, while they got sick and workers got sick and communities got sick. In only three months, the number of Covid-19 deaths in the United States was greater than the number of US troops killed during the Vietnam War.

The prison industry must come down. We can demand a moratorium on prison construction *today*. We can demand the defunding of police *today*. We can begin to decarcerate *today*.

We have witnessed the possibilities of abolition during Covid-19. During the pandemic, some incarcerated people were released based on their age, health, and chance of recidivism. The state also chose not to arrest and prosecute people for petty crimes. In the aftermath of the pandemic, we must sustain the same will to decarcerate. Just as the state made these moves to serve its own interests, we can continue them in the service of justice.

Of course, accountability should not be abandoned. Our communities must be protected from those who do harm. But we must ask challenging questions about the sources of the various forms of unsafety and harm we experience. We must also develop proactive measures to mitigate the harm we experience in our neighborhoods. Investment in mental health, conflict resolution, violence interruption—not to mention food, clothing, shelter, education, and living-wage jobs—are the starting point for addressing and preventing the various forms of suffering experienced by the vulnerable.

Within the United States, no vision of freedom can be discussed without reparations as a beginning. US empire was founded on the exploited labor of enslaved Africans. So much of our pain, our so-called pathologies, and our power-lessness is rooted in the institution of slavery. For this reason, the only way to even begin a conversation about justice for Black folk in the United States is with reparations for every single descendant of slavery.

We can no longer accept the longstanding arguments of the state that "we don't know who to give it to," "we can't afford it," or "we don't have the resources." As we learned during the economic shutdown that followed the pandemic, the government can always find the money, the resources, and the political will to do what was previously deemed im-possible. If we can find trillions to bail out the powerful, then we absolutely must do the same for the descendants of en-slaved African people.

The abolitionist imagination requires the capacity to en-vision an "impossible" future. Yes, a world without prisons and police seems impossible. But so did ending slavery, ac-cessing the vote, or ensuring marriage equality. Yet we have managed to achieve all of those things. When the people apply enough pressure, the state will bend. Not because it wants to, but because the people allow no other option.

The hard year of 2020 has shown us that anything is pos-sible. We can engage in political education. We can reshape our daily practices. We can reorient our ways of life. We can radically reorganize the world.

The challenge before us is to never relent. We cannot let our mission be coopted. We cannot reduce our radical vision to a reformist strategy. We cannot concede our right to reparations. We cannot settle for nicer occupiers or warmer cages. We cannot scale down our dreams. We cannot give up.

We Still Here.

Until victory. Always.

ABOUT THE COVER

During a protest over the death of George Floyd on Tuesday, June 2, 2020, demonstrators chant at Rittenhouse Square in Philadelphia (AP Photo/Matt Rourke). Lauren Coursey, pictured in the front of the crowd, offers this reflection on the moment captured:

I asked myself, "How did I end up leading over two thousand people through the streets of Philadelphia mimicking my chants?"

I couldn't stay home filled with rage even during a pandemic, witnessing how the narrative was playing out.

I needed to express my disappointment with our government and be in solidarity with the movement.

When I saw what happened to George Floyd and Breonna Taylor, I saw all the men and women in my life that I love so dearly that could be taken from me.

I had to do something, anything, to encourage the momentum in this movement, so this country isn't the same for myself and people who look like me.

Hopefully the children don't have to follow in my footsteps, proclaiming to others that their lives matter.

Will they hear us?

I don't know if they will, but it's life or death, so I have to try.

Say their names!

ABOUT THE AUTHOR

Marc Lamont Hill is the Steve Charles Professor of Media, Cities, and Solutions at Temple University. He is the author of five books, including *Beats, Rhymes, and Classroom Life*, *The Classroom and the Cell* (with Mumia Abu-Jamal), and the *New York Times* bestseller *Nobody: Casualties of America's War on the Vulnerable, From Ferguson to Flint and Beyond*. He is the host of *BET News* and the *Coffee & Books* podcast. Hill is the owner of Uncle Bobbie's Coffee & Books in Philadelphia.

ABOUT THE EDITOR

Frank Barat is a French activist, author, and film producer. He was the coordinator of the Russell Tribunal on Palestine from 2008 until 2014. He is the editor of *Gaza in Crisis* and *On Palestine* by Noam Chomsky and Ilan Pappé, *Freedom Is a Constant Struggle* by Angela Y. Davis, and *Défier le récit des puissants* by Ken Loach. He was part of the founding team of the Festival Ciné-Palestine in Paris and the Palestine with Love festival in Brussels and is the host of *Covid-19 Chronicles*.